77600262282

2.662 K643c
ssling, Elizabeth
veda.
pitalizing on the curse
the business of

CAPITALIZING ON THE CURSE

CAPITALIZING ON THE CURSE

The Business of Menstruation

Elizabeth Arveda Kissling

LYNNE
RIENNER
PUBLISHERS

BOULDER
LONDON

o 62161220

Published in the United States of America in 2006 by
Lynne Rienner Publishers, Inc.
1800 30th Street, Boulder, Colorado 80301
www.rienner.com

and in the United Kingdom by
Lynne Rienner Publishers, Inc.
3 Henrietta Street, Covent Garden, London WC2E 8LU

© 2006 by Elizabeth Arveda Kissling. All rights reserved by the publisher

Library of Congress Cataloging-in-Publication Data
Kissling, Elizabeth Arveda.
    Capitalizing on the curse : the business of menstruation /
Elizabeth Arveda Kissling.
    p.   cm.
    Includes bibliographical references and index.
    ISBN-13: 978-1-58826-310-0 (hardcover : alk. paper)
    ISBN-10: 1-58826-310-X (hardcover : alk. paper)
    1. Menstruation—Economic aspects—United States. 2. Menstruation—
Social aspects—United States. 3. Sanitary supply industry—United States—
History. 4. Sanitary napkins—United States—History. 5. Tampons—
United States—History. I. Title.
QP263.K57 2006
612.6'62—dc22   2005030836

British Cataloguing in Publication Data
A Cataloguing in Publication record for this book
is available from the British Library.

Printed and bound in the United States of America

The paper used in this publication meets the requirements
of the American National Standard for Permanence of
Paper for Printed Library Materials Z39.48-1992.

5 4 3 2 1

Contents

Figures and Tables

Figures

Tables

Acknowledgments

ALTHOUGH MINE IS THE ONLY NAME ON THE COVER, I RECEIVED assistance and support from many others in researching and writing this work. I would first like to acknowledge the students, friends, and colleagues who have sent me clippings and videotapes over the years. Lynne Rienner and the editorial staff at Lynne Rienner Publishers were enthusiastic and supportive of the project from the beginning. I am especially grateful to Bridget Julian, Lisa Tulchin, and Leanne Anderson. Mimi Marinucci, Chris Bobel, and Shawn Beard read the manuscript at different stages and offered invaluable suggestions and critiques, as did two anonymous reviewers for Lynne Rienner. Their insights made me a better writer and *Capitalizing on the Curse* a better book. None of these people, however, should be held accountable for the book's flaws and shortcomings; those are my responsibility alone. Every effort was made to contact the copyright holders for permission to use the figures presented in this book. In the event of an omission, please notify the author through Lynne Rienner Publishers.

I also received support from people who haven't read this work yet: my parents, Bill and Trudi Kissling; my sister, Mary Catherine; and my brother, Will, have been steadfast in their encouragement and confidence in me. And once again, I am thankful most especially to Doug Mitchell for all his endfull helpless advice, and for everything else.

—*Elizabeth Arveda Kissling*

Introduction:
From Rags to Riches

IN SPITE OF ALL THE SOCIAL, POLITICAL, AND ECONOMIC GAINS
women made in the twentieth century, taboos still limit women's
activities and public communication about menstruation. It is accept-
able to discuss menstruation only in highly limited and circumscribed
ways, such as complaining about menstrual symptoms, mocking
menstruating women, or helping to sell something related to menstruation. In these contexts, menstruation is either an illness to be
managed or a hygienic crisis to be cleaned up and hidden. Constru-
ing menstruation as a *problem* creates the possibility of, and perhaps
more importantly, a consumer market for, *solutions*—which begs a
variety of questions. Why is menstruation still a secret in a modern
society that claims to promote equality? How do women manage
menstrual needs while maintaining this secrecy? How is secrecy
maintained? What role does media play in keeping the secret? Who
benefits from the commercialization? Who benefits from the
secrecy? And ultimately, what does this mean for women in our society today?

The so-called feminine hygiene industry—at less than 100 years
old, a relatively recent development in the history of menstruation—
annually exceeds $2 billion in US sales (MarketResearch.com, 2001).
This figure does not include sales of such products as over-the-
counter or prescription remedies for menstrual pain or premenstrual
syndrome (PMS), nor the monies spent on advertising any of these
other menstruation-related products.

As menstruation is frequently defined as a medical event, even a
pathological one (Lander, 1988; Martin, 1987), the pharmaceutical
industry has recently developed products to "treat" menstruation or

its effects, and in doing so clears a profit. In its first few months of availability, $8 million worth of prescriptions were written for Sarafem (Gadsby, 2001), the antidepressant treatment for premenstrual dysphoric disorder (PMDD). Seasonale, the extended-use contraceptive introduced in 2003, is expected to have even greater sales. Barr Laboratories, the manufacturer of Seasonale, commissioned a 250-person sales force in late 2003 to promote the drug to physicians and healthcare providers (Barr Laboratories, 2003). Advertisements and other publicity for these products have become part of the public discourse about menstruation.

Menstruation is both a biological event and a cultural event; the biology cannot be separated from the culture, and neither is a predetermined category with consistent impact on individual women's lives. Interpretation of menstruation, whether by scientists, medical doctors, social scientists, or the women and girls who experience it, is always ideological (Lander, 1988). Indeed, how a society deals with menstruation may reveal a great deal about how that society views women.

My argument for the significance of menstruation, and thus my analysis of the discourses of menstruation, is grounded in Simone de Beauvoir's existentialist feminism. Although her classic feminist text, *The Second Sex*, is sometimes misunderstood as an outdated or even biased sociological treatise (Evans, 1998; Vintges, 1996), Beauvoir's analysis of the condition and status of women is firmly rooted in the existentialist philosophy that humans have no fixed nature, or essence—an idea that also undergirds much of contemporary postmodern theorizing about gender (e.g., Butler, 1989, 1990). Each of us creates our own identity, through our daily actions and the choices we make; contrary to Freudian and other psychoanalytic perspectives, biology is *not* destiny. Beauvoir's most famous line, "one is not born, but rather becomes, a woman" (1952: 301), is more than a simple statement of the social construction of gender. Enculturation is not a passive process but an achievement. For Beauvoir, *to become* is to make oneself into; to become a gender—whether feminine, masculine, or something else entirely—involves not merely submitting to a cultural situation, but also creating one (Atack, 1998; Evans, 1998). Much of *The Second Sex* is concerned with delineating the processes by which individuals internalize and adopt cultural norms they did not create (Atack, 1998); in other words, it details the process of "becom[ing] one's gender in a cultural context in which one is not, really, free to become much of anything else" (Butler, 1989: 257).

Beauvoir was among the very first feminist scholars to examine the ways in which women are *represented*. At the same time, Beauvoir remained cognizant of the materiality of the body: "the body being the instrument of our grasp upon the world, the world is bound to seem a different thing when apprehended in one manner or another" (1952: 36). Consistent with her existentialist worldview, Beauvoir regarded the body as a situation rather than a thing, and therefore its meaning is not fixed.

> It is not merely as a body, but rather as a body subject to taboos, to laws, that the subject is conscious of himself and attains fulfillment—it is with reference to certain values that he evaluates himself. And, once again, it is not upon physiology that values can be based; rather, *the facts of biology take on the values that the existent bestows upon them.* (1952: 40–41, emphasis added)

With its combination of feminism, materiality, and tolerance of ambiguity, Beauvoir's existentialist feminism is an ideal lens for examining cultural attitudes toward menstruation.

It is well documented that current attitudes toward menstruation in the United States are characterized by ambivalence and social discomfort (Houppert, 1999; Martin, 1987; Research & Forecasts, 1981; Roberts et al., 2002). Close examination of communication about menstruation reveals how these discourses contribute to the ongoing media construction of women as Other.

In the introduction to *The Second Sex*, Beauvoir wrote that the idea of the Other is "as primordial as consciousness itself" (1952: xix); the duality of Self and Other is a fundamental category of human thought. Alterity (the state of Otherness) is not inherently attached to women, but is an artifact of a male-dominated society in which the structures of law, economics, and social life work against women's ability to claim authentic subjectivity. Beauvoir described how numerous processes of socialization in patriarchal societies cultivate in women an alienation from their own bodies. A properly socialized woman develops a sense of herself as object, an Other that is both venerated and feared, as she internalizes her society's dominant ideologies about women.

Beauvoir's theory of woman as Other explains how woman is defined and differentiated only in terms of her relationship to man. Because man defines himself as human, as Subject, and woman is relative to man, she is Other. Each group tries to define itself by assigning traits it does not possess—or does not wish to possess—to the Other. Woman's position as Other is historically created and socially maintained—and thus difficult to escape (Lundgren-Gothlin, 1996).

Consistent with existentialist thought, the Other is woman's *situation*, not her essence. The claim of woman as the absolute Other does not mean every woman is only Other, all the time; "but rather that it characterizes women's general situation" (Lundgren-Gothlin, 1996: 173). This situation is a cultural creation, maintained by law, customs, and institutions. Members of the culture internalize these definitions and adopt them as their own (Beauvoir, 1952) and also resist them.

Beauvoir's detailed analyses of literary and cultural constructions of "the Eternal Feminine" (1952: 286) show how flesh-and-blood women struggle both to conform and to resist this identification. Although Beauvoir believes that everyone is capable of becoming a Subject, doing so requires freedom and self-determination. To become a Subject, one must believe oneself a Subject. To do so, one must live as a transcendent Subject, and when women in patriarchal societies assert their own transcendence, they are regarded as unfeminine (Lundgren-Gothlin, 1996).

Beauvoir briefly discusses the role of menstruation in these processes, noting that menstrual blood is often interpreted as the essence of femininity and thus as further justification of objectification of women. However, Beauvoir asserts that although biology is important, it is not "a fixed and inevitable destiny" (p. 36). While the body is "the instrument of our grasp upon the world," biological facts are "insufficient for setting up a hierarchy of the sexes; they fail to explain why woman is the Other; they do not condemn her to remain in this subordinate role forever" (p. 36). The biological facts are largely irrelevant; it is existence that defines woman. Because the body is a situation, rather than a thing, it is inherently unstable. The social construction of menstruation as a woman's curse is explicitly implicated in the evolution of woman as Other: "the blood, indeed, does not make woman impure; it is rather a sign of her impurity" (p. 169). That is to say, menstruation does not make woman the Other; it is because she is Other that menstruation is a curse.

> Just as the penis derives its privileged evaluation from the social context, so it is the social context that makes menstruation a curse. The one symbolizes manhood, the other femininity; and it is because

femininity signifies alterity and inferiority that its manifestation is met with shame. (1952: 354)

Discourses of menstruation in media and popular culture more than fifty years after Beauvoir wrote these words continue to reflect and reinforce woman's alterity. Messages about shame, secrecy, pollution, and Otherness lurk just below the surface even in seemingly progressive messages. For example, Ann Treneman (1989) has analyzed how advertisements for pads and tampons sell shame along with the product. Often they give the appearance of breaking menstrual taboos by speaking openly about the management of menstruation even as they promote its concealment. In advertisements for "feminine protection" the products are never shown in bathrooms, the room they are usually kept and used in; they are never shown in or after use; and blood is never shown or even mentioned. Such ads and their rules help to perpetuate the secrecy and shame surrounding menstruation (Treneman, 1989). The very term *feminine protection,* used *only* in advertising, implies menstruation is something that women (or their clothing) must be saved from.

In our postmodern era, a woman's relationship to her menstrual cycle is mediated through consumerism. That is, menstruation provides an opportunity for participation in consumer culture: Remedies for the illness of menstruation are bought and sold, as are means of coping with the hygienic crisis.

Capitalizing on the Curse explores representations of menstruation in US mass media and consumer culture from a feminist critical perspective informed by Beauvoir's feminist existentialism. A material-semiotic approach is used to examine these discourses, recognizing that "representation does not supersede materiality nor does materiality supersede representation" (Tuana, 1996). The analytic method is interdisciplinary, drawing upon my training in feminist cultural studies, speech communication, and folklore studies, and generally follows Stuart Hall's model of cultural analysis in three interconnected phases: (1) close, textual analysis of cultural material; (2) consideration of the effects of the cultural material on the society; and (3) placement of the material in its specific social and cultural contexts to produce an interpretation of cultural meaning and significance (Hall, n.d.).

The cultural texts I have chosen to examine here include print and television advertisements, films, episodic television programs, magazine articles, websites, and corporate press releases. They constitute what social scientists call a convenience sample; that is, most were selected for easy availability rather than by systematic searching or random sampling. Most of these cultural artifacts are not indexed and are difficult to locate any other way.[1] Many are from my own serendipitous searching and collecting, but I am also fortunate to have had numerous friends, students, and colleagues send me clippings and videotapes over the years.

I argue that these cultural texts about menstruation reinforce and even help create negative attitudes toward menstruation, toward women, and toward women's bodies, and that these attitudes are exploited to enhance corporate profits. I find the cultural meanings of menstruation to be intertwined with consumerism in numerous and often paradoxical ways. Consumption both constrains and empowers women (Miles, 1998; Lury, 1996). In popular discourses of menstruation, women are sold products that will liberate them from the perceived bonds of cyclic menstruation. This mind-set is so pervasive that it appears natural and undeniable. Even much of the emerging menstrual counterculture, while promoting alternative attitudes to the view of menstruation as an illness or hygiene crisis, still offers solutions through shopping.

The first two-thirds of the book presents some of the ways menstruation is imbued with consumerism. Chapter 2 examines the most well-known depictions of menstruation in mass media: feminine hygiene ads. These advertisements are part of the larger cultural narrative of ads directed toward women that instruct in how to maintain idealized femininity while concealing biological evidence of femaleness.

Chapter 3 scrutinizes those occasional moments in entertainment television and film when the arrival of a daughter's first period generates a few laughs. Some might argue that mention of menstruation in these venues at all is a progressive step for women and for minimizing menstrual taboos. Though my first inclination was to agree, critical examination of these depictions revealed them to be both reflective of and contributive toward a profound cultural gender bias that contributes to the collective definition of woman as Other.

Chapter 4 examines the disputes surrounding the creation of a new category of mental illness in the *Diagnostic and Statistical Manual of Mental Disorders* based on menstruation. It is argued that the impetus behind the creation of premenstrual dysphoric disorder was to increase the market for fluoxetine hydrochloride (originally patented as Prozac and recently patented as Sarafem for the treatment of PMDD) and other psychotropic drugs. Defining a normal part of female menstrual cycles as mental illness has the potential to label all women as mentally ill and perpetuates the dangerous trend of allowing pharmaceutical companies to define what counts as disease.

Chapter 5 addresses another pharmaceutical product designed to profit from distaste and shame about the menstrual cycle: Seasonale, an extended-cycle oral contraceptive that suppresses menstruation. Direct-to-consumer advertisements promote the drug not for its contraceptive effectiveness but for what is arguably a side effect: "Fewer periods. More possibilities." The possibilities include higher risk of breast cancer, osteoporosis, heart attacks, and stroke, but these are minimized in the drug's aggressive marketing campaign.

Chapter 6 considers the questions about dioxin and other contaminants in feminine hygiene products and examines the discourses of these debates. Promotional materials from major tampon manufacturers as well as those of makers of alternative products are examined. The final third of the book, in the second half of Chapter 6 and in Chapter 7, presents alternatives to the consumerist, corporate definitions of menstruation.

Chapter 7 looks to counterculture expressions regarding menstruation for alternative means of understanding and talking about menstruation. Harry Finley's online Museum of Menstruation is reviewed, along with Geneva Kachman's campaign to celebrate menstruation with her development of an original holiday, Menstrual Monday, and her own virtual museum. The emerging popularity of Vinnie's Tampon Cases is also evaluated. In Chapter 8, I offer strategies for building on the successes of this "menstrual underground" to transform cultural meanings and to become, in the existentialist sense, authentic menstruating subjects.

Note

1. It is rarer still for these items, particularly television and film products, to be indexed for menstruation-related content.

2

Marketing Menstruation

THERE IS NO SHORTAGE OF BLOOD IN US MASS MEDIA: NEWS broadcasts nightly reveal the blood of violent conflict; movies display gallons of simulated blood in simulated explosions and attacks; hit television shows vividly portray the treatment and investigation of blood-borne illnesses and gunshot wounds; and so on. But menstrual blood is never seen and seldom mentioned; acknowledgment of the fact that women menstruate remains rare. Menstruation is our "dirty little secret."

Even in the one domain of mass media where menstruation is regularly addressed—menstrual product advertising—menstruation remains hidden. Many scholars have asserted the importance of examining advertisements closely and taking their messages seriously, as advertising is a powerful ideological realm with sociocultural consequences beyond the corporate bottom line (Goldman, 1992; Kilbourne, 1999; McAllister, 1996; Williamson, 1978). Given that advertising for menstrual products is one of the few visible, public discourses about menstruation, it is especially important to examine messages about menstruation in mass-market ads. These texts implicitly and explicitly emphasize its dirtiness and/or its secrecy, and thus contribute to the ongoing cultural construction of women as Other.

That Not-So-Fresh Feeling

Although anthropologists Buckley and Gottlieb (1988) have convincingly asserted that "[t]he 'menstrual taboo' as such does not exist" (p. 7), one wouldn't know this from US advertisements for menstrual products. Buckley and Gottlieb explain that "what is found in close cross-cultural study is a wide range of distinct rules for conduct regarding menstruation that bespeak quite different, even opposite, purposes and meanings" (p. 7). In US advertisements, however, menstruation has a very limited set of purposes and meanings. These meanings frequently appear to be tied to older anthropological notions of menstruation as pollution or contamination. The legendary anthropologist Mary Douglas (1966) wrote that "our pollution behavior is the reaction which condemns any object or idea likely to confuse or contradict cherished classifications" (p. 37). In the world of menstrual product ads, the cherished ideal of femininity is contradicted by menstruation, and menstrual products are positioned as the only means of restoring clean, pure femininity. Femininity is tainted by menstruation, the visible sign of woman's status as Other, but as Beauvoir noted, menstruation is not the cause of her alterity, it is merely a sign of it. In other words, menstruation does not make women impure or dirty; they menstruate because they are dirty or impure. Because such uncleanliness cannot be stopped or prevented, it must be hidden.

Women have probably always used some form of bandage or tampon, although these devices have not always been mass produced or commercially available, nor have these products always been advertised. The first commercially available disposable menstrual product in the United States was "Lister's Towels," produced by Johnson & Johnson in 1896. These cotton pads covered in gauze were probably considerably more comfortable than the flannel diapers most women used at that time (Delaney, Lupton, and Toth, 1988). Early disposable pads were marketed primarily to a small number of women with disposable incomes; most women made their own menstrual rags well into the twentieth century, often from fabric sold expressly for that purpose (Park, 1996). Tampax tampons, the first commercially available tampons, were not developed and marketed until the early 1930s (Delaney, Lupton, and Toth, 1988; Houppert, 1999). However, the first disposable pads were not commercially successful, as contemporary mores restricted advertising and promotion of such products. It wasn't until the 1920s, when advertising executive Albert Lasker developed the strategy of placing coin containers in drugstores near the display of discreetly wrapped boxes of Kotex, so that women could just put money in the container and take the pads without having to ask for them, that disposable pads began to have any commercial success (Weiner, 2004).

Today, the feminine hygiene industry is highly competitive. Marketers and manufacturers have discovered that brand loyalty for menstrual products is strong and that a customer attracted in adolescence is likely to remain a customer for 35 or more years (Kaye, 2001). This is an important factor in marketing, as the Coalition of Brand Equity estimates that it costs six times as much money to win over a new customer than to keep a current one (Satish and Sri, 2005).

This is also why the industry has assumed responsibility for menstrual education in public schools. In the Victorian era, young girls of the middle class were often given health and hygiene manuals and expected to read to learn about menstruation, while working-class girls learned about menstruation from mothers, sisters, and female coworkers (Brumberg, 1997). As the menstrual products industry grew and established educational divisions as part of its marketing strategy, however, the industry gained more influence over menstrual education by supplying mothers, teachers, parent-teacher associations, and Girl Scout troops with free instructional materials about menstruation (Brumberg, 1997). These brochures, films, and free samples of products were gratefully received, but without awareness of the gradual shift in focus they introduced into how girls comprehend menstruation. For earlier generations, menstruation was understood in terms of its role in fertility; when the *femcare* industry—as it refers to itself—became the key provider of menstrual education, menstruation came to be seen as primarily a hygienic issue.

One may be tempted to minimize the influence of femcare ads, given that they top nearly everyone's list of most hated commercials. One trade publication reports that 41 percent of women find femcare ads, by definition, to be "in bad taste" ("Advertising: That's Very Interesting," 1994). But as noted above, advertising is a powerful sociocultural discourse, with influence equal to or greater than that of other ideological institutions (Kane, 1997). Ads are also influential for their ubiquitousness: Approximately 70 percent of US newspapers and 40 percent of mail consist of advertising, and the average US lifespan includes three years of watching television commercials—just the commercials (Kilbourne, 1999). As Jean Kilbourne says, "advertising is our environment. We swim in it as fish swim in water" (1999: 57). When the subject of the advertisements is one around which there is a great deal of ambivalence, it is easier for advertisers to interpret culture for consumers.

The primary goal of marketing and advertising, of course, is to convince the consumer that they need a particular product. Persuading the consumer that a particular product best meets this need when there is little product differentiation is an even greater challenge. As a product director at Johnson & Johnson's (manufacturers of Stayfree pads and o.b. tampons) Montreal office explained to an interviewer, "a pad is a pad is a pad" (Martin, 2002). Williamson (1978) asserts that it is in fact "the first function of an advertisement to create a differentiation between one particular product and others in the same category" (Williamson, 1978). Emphasizing bargain prices is seldom an option in the oligopolistic femcare market; there are only four major companies that market pads and tampons in the United States, so reducing prices in competition with one another just reduces revenue shares for all four. Instead, they compete to increase sales by building distinct brand identity.

Advertisers usually strive to create a differentiation by focusing on social meanings rather than merits of a product. Typically, these foci are fun, sexuality, wealth, health, and status (Scott, 2001). In menstrual ads, the focus is on "freshness" and how the product offered will preserve it against the threat posed by menstruation. In these ads, menstruation is always a problem. It is a hygiene crisis that one must clean up, in secret, so that one's public projection of ideal femininity is not damaged or polluted.

The feminine ideal has a long history in US media and advertising. Advertising has been targeted largely toward women since its development in the early twentieth century (Hill, 2002; Sivulka, 1998). One of the early guides for marketing to women emphasized the importance of framing its audience "not simply as workers and producers, but as *consumers*" (Christine Frederick, quoted in Mattelart, 1986, emphasis in original). Advertising of this early era tried to instill in women a feeling of control and knowledge as defined by the marketplace (Mattelart, 1986).

Concurrent with the larger hygiene movement of the 1920s, advertising for many products began to focus on cleanliness and frame numerous products as a means of avoiding embarrassment from inadequate personal hygiene. These ads not only shaped US habits, such as daily bathing and use of underarm deodorant, but influenced popular culture as well. For instance, the common saying "often a bridesmaid but never a bride" originated in a 1925 ad for Listerine "breath deodorant" (Sivulka, 1998).

Kane (1997) points out that the very existence of a category of products labeled "feminine hygiene" transmits a belief that women are dirty and in need of special cleansing products. Perhaps this recognition is the origin of the industry's euphemism for menstrual products, "femcare": It's better to imply their products care for femininity or feminine needs than that they clean up femininity. Kane asserts that commercials for feminine hygiene products "are in a unique position to articulate this culture's conception of femininity" (1997: 294).

In another study of femcare advertisements, Berg and Block Coutts (1994) specify the ideology of femininity portrayed in such ads. They also note that advertising in general strives to convince consumers that they need a particular product and thus frequently must work to create a need first. According to femcare ads, menstruation induces a state of tainted femininity—along with a fear of menstrual discovery. The products in question help maintain or restore "freshness," an undefined yet seemingly essential characteristic of femininity.

Femcare ads have also long emphasized the importance of secrecy; both menstruation and menstrual products must be concealed. When Kotex disposable napkins were first marketed, these early ads promised to "eliminate those tell-tale lines" (Treneman, 1989) and "that conspicuous bulkiness so often associated with old-fashioned methods" (Ad*Access On-Line Project, Ad #BH0019) as well as to help free women from "the possibility of offending others at times" (Ad*Access On-Line Project, Ad #BH0017). A 1924 ad promised a solution to "woman's oldest hygienic problem" (Ad*Access On-Line Project, Ad #BH0238). Such ads promote an increased menstrual awareness, as well as the development of the concept of menstrual odor, referred to obliquely in these ads and explicitly in later ads. Disposable, modern menstrual products were thus situated as more hygienic than older methods as advertisers simultaneously sought to exploit women's anxiety about causing offense to others. Other products to quash vaginal odor soon emerged as well. During the first half of the twentieth century, ads for Lysol, now marketed exclusively as a household disinfectant, promoted the cleaning solution's miraculous effects as a douche, sure to cure "marital problems."

The earliest tampon ads emphasized the freedom permitted to women, as well as a greater level of personal hygiene, with this new, medically approved menstrual product. Tampons were marketed as a revolutionary technological innovation that would free women from the bondage of belts, pins, and pads; allow women to transcend their menstrual cycle and become physically active every day of the month; and keep them from ever again being embarrassed by visible belt or pad lines or by menstrual odor (Park, 1996). A 1936 ad in *New York American Weekly* declared, "All the world is talking of this new emancipation of women. A new type of sanitary protection worn internally." It assured readers that "Tampax is hygienic, [and] sanitary, making daintiness possible at all times" (Ad*Access On-Line Project, Ad #BH0229). Early tampon ads were in an ideal position to exploit the sense of independence in women fostered by the recently passed Constitutional amendment granting women the right to vote. The emphasis on freedom and changing with the times also supported the role of women's magazines in cultivating the myth of modernity (Mattelart, 1986). For instance, a 1938 Tampax ad presents internal protection as "the civilized way," with "college girls lead[ing] the way in discovering" this "medically endorsed, revolutionary product" (Ad*Access On-Line Project, Ad #BH0159).

These twin themes of freedom and freshness remained dominant in ads for menstrual products. "Accent on freedom" headlined an ad for Modess in 1944, and in the 1970s, Johnson & Johnson named their beltless pads "Stayfree," while Kotex introduced a beltless pad named "New Freedom" (Hill, 2002). Like the well-known "You've Come A Long Way, Baby" campaign for Virginia Slims cigarettes, these ads for the 1970s products sought to capitalize on the burgeoning feminist movement by linking their product to women's emancipation. By the end of the century, however, the feminist angle had all but disappeared and ads featured a renewed emphasis on freshness (discussed in more detail below). A 2004 television ad for the latest version of Stayfree brand pads admonishes women to "stay clean, stay fresh, stay free."

Secrecy emerged mid-century as another central theme in tampon advertisements and remains a key message in menstrual ads. Some product lines were developed with concealment of the product (rather than merely concealment of menstruation) as their primary function. A tampon in the 1970s, Pursettes, was named for how easily it was concealed: a series of magazine ads in teen magazines of the era showed a comic strip of a girl accidentally spilling the contents of her purse, and a friend recommending the Pursettes brand for their ease of concealment in their stylish black carrying case (see Figure 2.1). Kotex followed suit with a similar product in the 1980s, with nonapplicator tampons individually wrapped in brightly colored opaque cellophane. Ads depicted the product as impossible for onlookers to identify. One showed an image of a young woman wearing them in her hair as curlers. A 2001 Tampax ad presented a new tampon,

Figure 2.1 Pursettes Advertisement, 1974

apparently developed explicitly for concealment. The Tampax "Compak" tampon's distinctive selling point is that it cannot be seen in a closed fist (see Figure 2.2). This theme of easy concealment was exaggerated for comic effect in a 2003 television commercial for Tampax. A teenage girl is caught passing a tampon to a classmate and

Figure 2.2 Tampax Compak Advertisement, 2001

Source: Used with permission of Procter & Gamble.

called to the front of the class, where the teacher examines the small, discreetly wrapped plug. He then looks the student in the eye and says, "I hope you brought enough for everyone!" The student chuckles and replies, "Enough for the girls."

The newest permutation of the secrecy theme emerged in 2004 in a television ad for a new Kotex product: the product's distinguishing feature is that it can be unwrapped silently, as the plastic wrapper is designed to be "crinkle-free." Unlike the female camaraderie suggested by the old Pursettes ads and the recent Tampax ads in which young women share products, this newer Kotex ad suggests women should hide their menstruation even from other women. This ad, along with Web advertising and the "Red Dot" campaign, is part of Kotex's new efforts to reach younger women (Leggiere, 2005). It's more than a little ironic to see this emphasis on secrecy from the company lauded for increasing openness about menstruation in its advertising. The Red Dot was introduced in television and print ads in 2000 as a symbol of a woman's *period,* playing on the word's meaning as both menstruation and a mark of punctuation. The ads showed a large red dot interrupting words like *vacation* and *weekend,* instead of appearing at the end of a sentence. The Red Dot ads were the first in the United States to use the word *period* and the first to feature the color red prominently. The campaign was regarded as innovative and clever within the advertising industry and praised by consumers for its frankness and humor (Leggiere, 2005; Weiner, 2004).

As Berg and Block Coutts (1994) point out, menstruation in the world of femcare ads invokes a complex system of menstrual management. One must keep menstruation concealed, to prevent one's carefully constructed front of femininity from becoming damaged by the taint of menstrual pollution. The variety of products necessary to manage this concealment has expanded throughout the twentieth century, although there have been few real innovations in menstrual products since disposable products first became commercially available. That is to say, although more products fill the shelves of the femcare aisle at supermarkets and discount stores, there is little meaningful diversity of products. Stick-on pads and mini-pads with temporary adhesive on the underside, eliminating the need for pins or special belts to hold sanitary napkins in place, replaced the older-style pads in the 1970s, and the 1980s brought "wings" to maxi-pads—small sticky tabs used to secure the pad to the underside of the wearer's panties. Disposability, internal protection, and ability to use without hardware are the most significant real improvements in menstrual products. Yet advertisements frequently promote the newest technologies of menstrual products, such as uniquely designed applicators, technically superior fibers, and specially shaped pads, as if they were real and significant innovations in menstrual care. Because capitalist systems require that needs change in order for the system to thrive, the frequent small changes in the products are promoted as accommodations to women's changing needs. Houppert (1999) lists some of the new menstrual products introduced in the last ten years: curved pads (Kotex), stay-put tabs (Kimberly-Clark), glossy cardboard applicators (Playtex and Tampax), lite [sic] tampons (Tampax), multipacks of tampons of varying absorbencies (Tampax), applicators for a formerly "applicator-free" brand (o.b.), and "four-walled protection" (Stayfree). In 2001, thong-shaped panty liners were introduced, to great success (Wallace, 2003). The same year also saw Procter & Gamble's Always line of pads add a special pad for large-sized women, defined as those who wear size 14 or above. The product name included the words "Maximum Protection," and the package promised "30% more panty coverage than regular pads." Many women found this product insulting, with its implication of the extra-large vagina that requires it. The plus-size fashion magazine *Grace* published a pithy opinion piece to that effect, asking why a special pad hasn't been developed for the woman size 6 or smaller, who by analogy must require an extra-narrow pad to accommodate her "teeny little vageeny" (Shanker, 2002: 50).

Freshness Versus Freedom

Few could dispute the assertion that these innovations in menstrual products increased women's freedom of movement, both physically and socially. It is hard for modern women to imagine women dancing—in close-fitting clothing, no less—or playing sports while wearing nineteenth-century cloth diapers or even the mid-twentieth-century bulky disposable pads held in place with elastic belts and metal clips. Although athletes and entertainers were the first women to use commercial tampons, as well as the first targeted markets, tampons made it considerably easier for women in all walks of life to play sports, dance, or engage in other demanding physical activities during all phases of the menstrual cycle.

The nature of modern menstrual products also facilitates their easy concealment. Most tampons are small enough to be carried discreetly when a woman only suspects that her period might arrive. Joan Benoit Samuelson, winner of the 1984 Olympic marathon, ran that historic race[1] with a "just-in-case" tampon in a baggie pinned inside her running shorts (Samuelson and Averbuch, 1995).

Although it is not often discussed in historical accounts of women in the workforce, availability of comfortable, discreet, affordable menstrual products has been a factor in increasing women's occupational and educational opportunities. Modern workplaces and schools typically have bathrooms available to women workers as private spaces to deal with menstrual needs, although this has certainly not always been the case—working and sanitary conditions in the nineteenth and early twentieth century were often horrific (Martin, 1987). Many public bathrooms have tampon dispensers, making it easy for a woman to purchase a single tampon or pad if her period arrives unexpectedly.[2] (Of course, menstrual supplies still must be purchased, calling to mind Gloria Steinem's [1978] speculation that if men menstruated, "supplies would be federally funded and free.")

This is not to say that it is always easy for women to manage their menstrual cycle in the workplace; cultural norms that restrict women's ability to be frank about menstrual pain or the need to change a pad or tampon complicate women's working lives. Women must find ways to take breaks away from workstations and locate or carry menstrual supplies without drawing undue attention to themselves, sometimes several times a day. This can be especially problematic for female students; several informants spoke to Emily Martin about the difficulty of managing menstruation in high school:

> "In school it's hard; teachers don't want to let you out of the classroom, they're upset if you're late and give you a hard time."
> "In seventh grade I didn't carry a pocketbook or anything—wow!—How do you stash a maxi-pad in your notebook and try to get to the bathroom between classes to change? It was like a whole procedure, to make sure nobody saw, that none of the guys saw. From your notebook and into your pocket or take your whole notebook to the ladies' room which looks absolutely ridiculous." (Two informants quoted in Martin, 1987: 93–94)

Martin (1987) points out that US workplaces are not compatible with women's reproductive lives in numerous ways—especially when compared to other industrialized nations. In her analysis of PMS (discussed further in Chapter 4), she noted that many effects of menstruation and premenstrual syndrome are not inherently negative but are seen as such because they are inconsistent with the requirements of work in our society (Martin, 1988).

Ironically, as menstrual products have become smaller and more discreet and menstruation has become easier to conceal, the demands for freshness portrayed in ads are continually ratcheted up. Images of women in menstrual product ads frequently show women wearing close-fitting white slacks, for instance. Early tampon ads touted the elimination of any potential for odor by the virtue of being worn internally, but by the 1970s, some tampon manufacturers began perfuming their products. A recent example can be seen in a 2003 magazine ad for Playtex deodorant tampons: A full-page image shows a laughing woman seated at a bar, interacting with two men. In the upper right corner of the page is a small inset photo of a seated infant wearing only a diaper and a clothespin on her nose. The phrase "Pads don't just feel like diapers" is at the top of the page, insinuating that menstrual blood smells like feces (Fudge, 2004). The newest product from Procter & Gamble, Tampax Fresh, promotes its fresh scent with a scratch-and-sniff magazine ad like those used to market perfume and cologne. The text invites readers to, "Beguile your senses. Succumb to the freshness." The ad's imagery so resembles a perfume ad, with a woman in a white gown posing in the shallow water of a beach with her face lifted to the sunset, that it fooled the student who brought it to my attention (Figure 2.3). (His befuddlement inspired me to quiz a few other people, showing them the page and asking if they could identify the product being sold. One of my guinea pigs assumed it was an ad for breath freshener. Another thought it was for a weight-loss product. None guessed that it was for a menstrual product.)

Femininity Isn't Female

This renewed marketing emphasis on scented tampons occurs in a cultural moment in which the aesthetic contrast between femininity and femaleness has never been greater. "One of the obligations that women have in a culture that sexually objectifies their bodies is to conceal the biological functioning of their bodies," asserts Tomi-Ann Roberts (2004: 22). For instance, the majority of women in Western countries remove leg and underarm hair to appear more feminine; the practice is so commonplace that it often goes unremarked, even in studies and analyses of women's body image (Tiggermann and Lewis, 2004). Methods of body hair removal proliferate in the twenty-first century, and removal of pubic hair is becoming an increasingly common behavior and expectation for young women.

Roberts proposes that menstrual concealment, like women's shaving practices and dieting behaviors, can be explained, in part, by objectification theory. That is, "the cultural milieu of sexual objectification functions to socialize girls and women to, at some level, treat themselves as objects to be evaluated based on appearance" (Roberts, 2004: 22). Or in John Berger's more succinct phrasing, "men *act* and women *appear*" (1973: 47, emphasis in original). Advertising is one of the cultural institutions that shapes this process; arguably, advertising

Figure 2.3 Tampax Fresh Advertisement, 2005

Beguile your senses
Succumb to the freshness.

Source: Used with permission of Procter & Gamble.

fulfills a social function today comparable to that of art or religion in previous eras. It is a modern form of cultural mythology, providing simple scripts and stories to guide behavior and convey values and beliefs (Dyer, 1988). The marketing of freedom, freshness, and fear of menstrual exposure in feminine hygiene advertisements is a visible instance of "mystification"—Beauvoir's label for the process that sustains inequitable relations between women and men by teaching women how to become the Other. In purchasing and using these products, women are compelled to buy into the idea of the menstruating woman as somehow tainted and internalize their own Otherness.

Notes

1. 1984 was the first year women were permitted to compete in the Olympic marathon.

2. I am assuming that the tampon dispenser in the women's room at my workplace, with its coin slot reading "EMPTY" for the entire twelve years I have worked there, is an anomaly.

3

Blood On-Screen

AS IT IS IN ADVERTISING, IN THE WORLDS REPRESENTED IN FILM
and television, menstruation, when it occurs at all, is a crisis. Menarche, a girl's first period, is portrayed more frequently than ordinary menstruation and is nearly always portrayed as a crisis, for both the menstruating girl and her anxious, well-intentioned parents. Film representations are typically brief scenes that mark the arrival of menarche and the beginning of a female character's indoctrination into the practices of menstrual concealment (examples include *My Girl, Angel at My Table, A Walk on the Moon, Carrie*). However, menarche has been portrayed with more diversity and less conventional indoctrination in recent television comedies (*Blossom, The Cosby Show, Roseanne, Something So Right, Everwood*). Because films and television programs are not explicitly selling products, they have greater freedom to vary the menarche script. Some of these programs even attempt a reframing of menarche, as they show parents struggling to mark their daughter's first period in a positive way.[1]

Menstruation at the Movies

Menarche is seldom a focus of a movie or even a minor plot line. Typically, the arrival of a character's first period is a relatively brief scene used to illustrate a larger point. For example, in *My Girl* (1991), Vada's first period serves as a symbolic marker of her evolution from tomboy to adolescent girl. Raised by a single father in the early 1970s, Vada is unprepared for menarche and something of a hypochondriac, so the sight of her first menstrual blood frightens her;

she believes she is hemorrhaging and will soon die of cancer. She runs through the house yelling for her father, but he is not at home. Instead, his girlfriend/employee, Shelly, takes Vada aside and explains menstruation and sexual intercourse to her off-camera. Vada exclaims, "It's not fair! Nothing happens to boys." The doorbell interrupts their conversation, and Vada, suspecting it is her best friend Thomas J. and not in the mood to see any boys, goes to the door and tells Thomas to "Go away! And don't come back for five to seven days!"

The menarche scene in *My Girl* represents a turning point in Vada's development and in the movie. It is a concrete realization for Vada that she is a girl, will develop into a woman, and must abandon her childhood pastimes. It also represents a turning point in Vada's relationship with Shelly. This is their first interaction, since her dad began dating Shelly, in which Vada is not antagonistic to her. It is also Shelly's first "mothering" action toward Vada, and it foreshadows their future relationship as stepmother and stepdaughter. For Vada the tomboy, it is an epiphanal moment of recognition that boys and girls really are different.

On a more subtle level, Vada's rejection of Thomas J. perhaps illustrates a desire for menstrual seclusion; some believe it is quite common for menstruating women to crave time alone for rest and rejuvenation, perhaps even unconsciously (Pope, 2001). Vada is beginning to pull away from her male best friend as she becomes a woman. It is also noteworthy that Thomas J.'s suggested activity for the day is swimming, a common menstrual taboo. This serves as another message to Vada that her life must change now that she is a woman. Note also the implicitness of this representation: The words *menstruation* and *period* are never uttered, and no blood appears on-screen.

The (in)famous menarche scene in *Carrie* (1976), in which the title character is pelted with tampons in the girls' locker room, also marks a turning point in the main character's life. Like Vada in *My Girl*, Carrie had no prior knowledge of menstruation and thus was shocked and fearful when she discovered her first blood. Her mother, a pious and devout evangelical Christian, had not prepared Carrie for menstruation because she believed that it happened only to sinful women and that her daughter was free of sin. When Carrie arrives home angry with her mother for not preparing her, she is punished for sinning. Her relationship with her mother is forever changed. The primary story line, however, has more to do with another turning point: With the arrival of her first period, Carrie also acquires telekinetic powers, which she later uses to seek revenge on the classmates who have tormented her over the years.

The menarche scene in *A Walk on the Moon* (1999) also represents a turning point or epiphany, for the menstruating girl's mother as much as for herself. In this film, the main character is Pearl Kantrowitz, a woman who wonders what her life would be like had it not been overdetermined by early motherhood and marriage. At age 31 in the summer of 1969, she is on a family vacation in upstate New York with her husband, mother-in-law, young son, and adolescent daughter. With her husband working in the city during the week, Pearl finds herself tempted by the flirtations of the "Blouse Man," a traveling salesman who visits the campground weekly to sell his wares to the women. As Pearl becomes more intimate with the Blouse Man, her fourteen-year-old daughter, Alison, is experiencing many of the rites of passage common to female adolescents in the United States: first date, first kiss, first period, and first serious rebellion against parental authority.

Her menarche, and her responses to it, are shown in several scenes early in the film. Alison calls her Bubbe (grandmother), Lillian, into the family bathroom, and shows her the blood on her underpants. Lillian exclaims with a mixture of joy and pride, "Mazeltov!" She then slaps Alison across the face, repeating the once common tradition of some European and Jewish families.[2] Bubbe tells Alison that she never understood the tradition herself and in fact promptly returned her own mother's slap. Upon hearing this, Alison slaps her grandmother, and Lillian's shout attracts Pearl's attention. Pearl joins her daughter and mother-in-law in the tiny bathroom, and upon learning the reason for their agitation ("Pearl, I have news: Alison became a woman today"), she hugs and kisses her daughter. Later that day, as Pearl, Lillian, and another adult woman friend worry about Alison's seclusion, Alison emerges from the bungalow dressed for her first date. As she leaves, she asks her mother, "Please don't tell Daddy I got my period." The camera then centers on Pearl's face, for it is already too late for Alison's request. As the teen walks across the campground, she is paged for a long-distance phone call: "It's your father, Alison! You're a woman today. Mazeltov! May you be blessed with a happy marriage and many, many children!" Alison cringes, as female and male campers of all ages applaud her.

The menarche scenes in *A Walk on the Moon* are quite a bit longer than the menarche scenes in *My Girl* and *Carrie,* and they are qualitatively different as well. The initial image of Alison's panties is visually striking, brief as it is, for although it is not uncommon to see blood on-screen in US movies, it is rare to see explicit representation of menstrual blood. Alison is shown getting her period, telling her family, shopping for menstrual products with her best girlfriend (encountering the boys they are interested in at the drugstore), and experiencing two informal rituals welcoming her to the community of women (her grandmother's slap and the applause of the other campers). She is not unhappy about the event, although she does experience some embarrassment in the drugstore and on her way to the phone. Her family's response to her news is good wishes and happiness for her. Her friends and family do not emphasize shame and secrecy, and in fact they seem proud to share the news and even to celebrate menarche with her.

At the same time, these episodes emphasize difference between women and men, evidenced in the girls' concealment of the menstrual products from the boys, Alison's attempt to keep the news of her menarche from her father, and even in the emphasis on "becoming a woman." The acquisition of femininity must be concealed from men, as though that femininity itself were tainted.

Menarche is a sign, as in *My Girl* and other movies. In the larger narrative structure of this film, Alison's development is compared and contrasted with her mother's, as Pearl experiences her own sexual awakenings and rebellion against convention and authority. Thus, the irony of Lillian's line to Alison, "You see, meschenka, you become a woman and the world looks a little brighter."

In these films, menstruation and menarche work as an enthymeme, which encapsulates an implicit philosophical argument about the materiality of the body. The arrival of menstruation is a powerful reminder or signifier to these women that no matter what they do or say, or how they live their lives, they are still female and Other. This is especially dramatic for characters who have in some way violated conventional expectations of femininity or female behavior.

This is vividly portrayed in the teen horror film *Ginger Snaps* (2000). Sisters Brigitte and Ginger Fitzgerald are misfits in their high school, the kind of intellectual loners who are above the interests of jocks and cheerleaders and prefer it that way. Their latest project is staging and documenting a photo montage of 1001 ways to die, including hangings, decapitation, and other gory scenarios. The two are fascinated with death and have made a suicide pact together: "Out by sixteen or dead in this scene, but together forever."

Ginger Snaps is a werewolf movie with a twist. Late in the evening of the day of Ginger's first period (menarche is late for both girls, symbolic of their reluctance to join the adult world emulated by their peers), the sisters are attacked by a mysterious beast roaming their suburban neighborhood. Ginger is slowly transformed, from outcast to cool kid, from shy and virginal to promiscuous and blood-thirsty—literally. She becomes a werewolf, and lycanthropy becomes a metaphor for female adolescence (Oler, 2003). Menstruation makes her a monster. However, as Tammy Oler's insightful analysis argues, *Ginger Snaps* differs from the pervasive representation of female adolescence as monstrous in this subgenre of horror movies by offer-ing an existentialist feminist critique:

> As if to respond to the clichés that express an essential, biological link between femaleness and horror, *Ginger Snaps* entreats us to examine how potentially damaging such links are for young girls. The reluctance the sisters feel toward reaching puberty stems pre-cisely from their desire not to be reduced to their female parts. *Gin-ger Snaps* asserts instead that girls need not be empowered through anything specifically female—anything that derives from their essential biological capacities—but through their ability to express themselves as individuals. (Oler, 2003: 50–51)

Menstruation as mark of the Other is also seen in the film *Boys Don't Cry* (1999), a dramatic interpretation of the last year of Bran-don Teena's life. Menstruation, though not menarche, is an important signifier in this film. Brandon has been successfully presenting him-self as a man—so successfully that even the viewing audience is shocked when Brandon's period arrives. There is no on-screen dia-logue about menstruation, but we see Brandon waking up and dis-covering a blood stain in his jeans and furtively scrubbing them in the bathroom sink. Later, we see him stealing tampons from a con-venience store, and hiding the used applicators and wrappers under a mattress. Their later discovery by one of his new friends is part of the information that unravels his story and his identity, which leads to the ultimate punishment for violating gender norms and expecta-tions. Brandon was raped and murdered by some of these supposed friends, in real life and in the film, apparently in the belief that his gender portrayal was a betrayal.

Menstruation on the Small Screen

In the television representations, menarche plays a much larger role in each episode's plot line than it does in the plot lines of film repre-sentations. A daughter's first period, and more specifically, how her parents deal with it, is the focus of such episodes. Menarche becomes the problem in the conventional problem-solution narrative structure of television sitcoms and family dramas. As with children's problems in most domestic comedies (Taflinger, 1996), it is usually represented as a problem for the girl's parents, and only secondarily a problem for the menarcheal girl herself. As in film portrayals, menarche on television reinforces gendered behavior and gender difference.

In *Something So Right,* a 1990s situation comedy about the life of a blended family in Manhattan, the daughter's first period happens while she is at school, and when she returns home, only her stepfather and older brother are there to hear the news and to provide comfort. Her stepfather is at a loss but wants to do "the right thing," as he recognizes the importance of her menarche. He struggles to offer a verbal response, visibly stunned by her news. He offers an awkward high-five. He directs his stepson to get his mother on the phone immediately, as he explains the importance of this event: "Your sister will remember whatever I say and do tonight for the rest of her life" (Sheehan, 1998). The rest of the episode portrays Mom's struggle to leave an important, career-building event at work and her guilt at not being at home with her daughter for this important developmental moment. It is repeatedly emphasized that although Dad may do his best, he is no substitute for Mom at this critical moment. This is highlighted by the chastising of Dad's ex-wife, the mother of the oldest daughter in this blended family, for missing her daughter's menarche; it is mentioned in the script three times, by three different characters. The ex-wife expresses her regret and seems to overcompensate by providing an inventive, new-age ritual for her ex-husband's stepdaughter. Although he mocks this display and attempts to conceal it from his new wife, his menstruating stepdaughter expresses appreciation for the effort.

The apparent theme of this episode is how important it is for a mother to be at home with her children. Menarche becomes a crisis for the family because Mom is not there to share it. In trying to leave work early, the mother character plays on her client's sympathy and longing for an intimate mother-child relationship. He ends up driving her home and saying to her in the car, "This [home] is where you should be."

The perceived differences between women and men are a prominent theme in this program, as in most television sitcoms, exaggerated here in the feigned role reversal with Dad setting the table, preparing dinner, and looking after the children while Mom works late. As Philip Green (1998) noted, these sitcom role reversals are not as transgressive as they may seem; we perceive them as humorous only because we can't take them too literally. The comedy arises from the apparent distortion of reality—we laugh, because real men don't do housework.

We can see the same strategy in a 1999 episode of the animated comedy *King of the Hill* (Judge, 1999). Hank and Peggy Hill have no daughter but are looking after a neighbor's child while her parents are out of town. When her first period arrives, Hank is the only one available to help her. Unable to reach the girl's parents or Peggy, Hank rushes her to the local hospital's emergency room. Although Connie's "problem" is quickly diagnosed and a remedy prescribed, Hank's responsibilities are not over: He must take Connie to the store and face the dreaded Aisle 8A, where the menstrual supplies are stacked. Hank sends the girl down the aisle alone, begging her to hurry and find what she needs. When she panics at the mystery of choices and bursts into tears, Hank runs down the aisle and makes the selection for her. When she later asks how to use these new products, Hank panics, and has Peggy brought home from work by a police escort. He explains the situation to Peggy, who immediately takes over, but only after expressing her amazement that Hank faced Aisle 8A—in twenty years of marriage, she's never seen him pass Aisle 5.

Again, the source of humor is the role reversal: We are surprised to see a man deal with a girl's first period, and do so effectively, because that's not how it happens in "real life." Instead of disrupting the sex/gender system and family roles, such scenes reinforce cultural stereotypes. Both of these programs also displayed the availability of an ever-increasing number of menstrual hygiene products as a mystery to men, emphasizing male ineptitude in this clearly female realm. They also remind viewers that key developmental moments are always marked by consumer behaviors.

7th Heaven presents a superficially less-conventional portrayal of menarche. *7th Heaven* is the story of the Camden family: Dad is pastor of a Christian church, and Mom is full-time caretaker of their five (later seven, as the show developed over the years) children. In the series premiere, the middle child, Lucy, incidentally also the middle daughter, is eagerly awaiting her first period. The story of her imminent period is interwoven with three other plot lines involving other Camden family members (Hampton, 1996).

At twelve, Lucy fears she may never menstruate; she is already so late compared to her friends. She is cranky and irritable, especially with her father, who seems almost as eager for her period as she is. She asks her mother to "keep Dad out of this," then is mortified the next day when he opens his Sunday sermon with the same passage from Ecclesiastes that Mom used to comfort her ("To everything there is a season, a time for every purpose under the sun . . ."). Lucy runs from the church. Later, she and her fourteen-year-old sister Mary encounter a boy Mary is interested in, and Lucy accidentally knocks her "just in case" tampon out of her pocket. She again runs away, but Mary nonchalantly picks up the tampon and pockets it, then asks the boy, "So are you coming over or not?" Lucy's embarrassment and eagerness for menstruation are constantly juxtaposed, which heightens the contrast between Lucy and her more open older sister and her dad, who wants to share what he labels a "perfectly normal and wonderful process of becoming a woman." He uses this phrase in a private conversation with his wife, in which they are discussing Lucy's sensitivity and comparing the two daughters. Mom advises Dad to back off and lets him know that menstruation isn't quite as wonderful as he thinks it is.

Of course, Lucy's period eventually does arrive, and she is joyfully dancing with her two sisters when Dad walks in. He asks if congratulations are in order, and Lucy nods in confirmation. He offers to send Lucy, Mary, and Mom out to dinner, a special celebration for "just the women of the house." In spite of his earlier enthusiasm, it is clear to him that he must be excluded from this event.

Although the *7th Heaven* portrayal is complicit in the marking of the menstruating female as Other, it is unusual in several respects. First, it portrays a father so eager to share his daughter's first period that he longs to be sent to the drugstore for a "big blue box of slender regulars." Second, no other TV or film daughter is shown quite so eager for her first period. Third, the openness and lack of embarrassment surrounding menstruation for Dad and the fourteen-year-old sister are rare on-screen and off (Kissling, 1996b). These can be read as positive elements of an increasing social acceptance of menstruation and reduction in menstrual concealment taboos; however, they are undermined by the emphasis on Lucy's embarrassment and the role of menstruation in heightening awareness of female difference. *7th Heaven* is also unusual in that it has used a menarche plot line twice; by the summer of 2003, the show had been on the air long enough for the character of Lucy Camden's younger sister to reach menarche. Unlike her two older sisters, however, Ruthie was secretive about her first period and confided in neither parent.

In a 2005 episode of *Everwood,* we see another dad who is willing to talk about menstruation with a reluctant young daughter. *Everwood* is the story of a physician dad who has relocated his practice and his family from Manhattan to rural Colorado after the death of his wife. His daughter Delia is the star of and only girl on her hockey team. The scene in which she announces her just-discovered menarche shows her exiting the family bathroom and solemnly informing her older brother, "It's here." He asks, "What's here? An alien invasion? The Britney Spears tour?" She responds more slowly and loudly, "It's here." Her brother's sudden awareness prompts him to yell immediately for their father, revealing the teenage boy to be unprepared and unwilling to acknowledge, much less assist with, his sister's first period.

We then see Dad escorting Delia to the drugstore and inviting her to talk—he tells her he's got a speech prepared because this is one of the very few things he knew would happen. She doesn't want to talk about her period or listen to his speech; she is more focused on her upcoming hockey semifinals. Dad suggests maybe Delia would prefer talking with a woman and suggests their friend Nina. Delia again declines and wants to get her menstrual supplies and get out of the store. He seems as baffled by the product choices as she is and says, "Wings sound nice." Delia grabs the package, along with a couple of other packages of different products. Apparently his prepared speech contains no advice about how to use menstrual products.

Delia is later shown curled up in her bed, apparently ill from menstruating. She is determined, however, not to let down her team by missing the big game. However, when her dad pressures the coach to take it easy on her because she has her period, the coach's reply of apparent disgust is overheard by Delia's teammates. The coach removes Delia from the game, and the boys begin teasing her, telling her she should sit out the whole period (a weak hockey joke; probably funnier if you're eleven years old, as these characters are).

Delia is embarrassed and angry with her father for revealing her period to the entire hockey team but still won't discuss menstruation with him. He again offers her Nina and suggests his nurse would be another good alternative. He is dumbfounded when she finally says the only person she wants to talk to is her mother—who, by the way, would never have exposed her secret to the entire team. Throughout the episode, he is insistent that she must talk about menstruation with someone, even disclosing to his girlfriend his frustration that Delia refuses to discuss her period. The episode ends with Delia finally confiding in her brother's girlfriend and deciding to quit the hockey team.

Like *7th Heaven*, *Everwood* gives viewers mixed messages about menarche. Menstruation is not a secret here; we have adults eager and willing to talk about it openly with an adolescent girl, and Delia's "It's here" response suggests that she has already had conversations about menstruation within her family—even though her brother doesn't want to help her, he does know what it means. By the end of the episode, however, the transformative power of menarche to turn tomboys into girls has done its work: Delia has given up hockey, because she "just doesn't feel like playing" any more, and asked Amy for information about gymnastics—a sport stereotypically deemed feminine and more appropriate for girls.

Judging solely from anecdotal evidence, *The Cosby Show*'s 1990 "Woman's Day" episode is the most widely seen television menarche. This episode, officially titled "The Infantry Has Landed," is often praised for its positive portrayal of menstruation, probably because of Claire Huxtable's feisty response to her teenage son's friend's stereotypes about menstruation. She informs the young man that a woman is entitled to have any kind of mood she wants, whenever she wants, regardless of her menstrual status. Many viewers also seemed to appreciate the show's proposed celebration of menarche, "Woman's Day," in which the menstruating daughter selects an activity of her choice to share with her mother to celebrate the occasion. However, these messages are subtly undermined by the infrequent appearance of the menstruating daughter, as a competing plot line about the college-student son trying to use what he's learning in his "Theories of Personality" course to analyze his father is prominent. Although an early scene in the episode shows the girl's older sisters fondly reminiscing about their own "Woman's Day" celebrations with Mom, "The Infantry Has Landed" features no interaction between the menstruating daughter and her father. There were no awkward congratulations, no euphemistic conversations—Cliff and Rudy Huxtable's paths do not cross at all during the days surrounding her menarche. This is noticeably different from all of the other television episodes about menarche I have seen and a subtle sign that menstruation should be celebrated and discussed only with women, enforcing the secrecy message.

Menstruation was not a secret on *Roseanne*. As it did with several social issues during its 1988–1996 run, Roseanne's self-titled family comedy series offered an ideologically powerful message about menarche. In the episode of *Roseanne* titled "Nightmare on Oak Street" (McKeaney, 1989), Roseanne and Dan Connor's middle child, Darlene, gets her first period. Darlene is reluctant to acknowledge and accept menstruation, and the awkwardness of her parents, especially her father, further complicates this event for her. Darlene has always been a tomboy, who preferred the company of her father to that of her mother and sister and enjoyed participating in traditionally father-son activities with him. In this episode, they are working on a boat together. But Darlene claims to have lost interest, and she seems ambivalent about her upcoming basketball game.

The episode shows both of Darlene's parents struggling to acknowledge her period and new status in a way that will please her. Dan tries to assume little has changed, and he tries to involve her with the boat as before. When Darlene is reluctant, he awkwardly congratulates her and tries to say something fatherly and affectionate. Roseanne first talks with her sister, Jackie, about what to say to Darlene to try to make her first period as positive for her as she can. Roseanne says to Jackie that although Darlene may not feel like it now, "this is something to celebrate." Jackie doesn't agree and can think of little positive about menstruation. The two talk about how important it is to handle it differently than their mother, who advised them that if they had any questions, they should ask the school nurse. This is quite realistic dialogue, as mothers I have interviewed about preparing their daughters for menarche made similar comments (Kissling, 1996a).

When Roseanne finally talks to her daughter, we see a rare moment of counterideological television—that is, an instance of televisual culture that acknowledges some of the underlying but often unpleasant realities of conflict and contradiction (Green, 1998). It offers a marked contrast to the other portrayals of menarche. Roseanne enters Darlene's bedroom and finds her throwing away all of her sporting equipment, which she apparently thinks is no longer appropriate now that she is a woman. But Roseanne encourages her to keep them because she loves them and because they *are* a woman's things—as long as a woman uses them. Roseanne explains that there are lots of ways to be a woman and that Darlene can choose the kind of woman she wants to be; she doesn't have to wear makeup and dresses and spend time at the mall like her older sister. She also tries to counter Darlene's sense of tainted femininity, telling her daughter that she is lucky: "Now you get to be part of the whole cycle of things—the moon, and the water and the seasons. It's almost magical, Darlene. You should be really proud today because this is the beginning of a lot of wonderful things in your life."

Roseanne presents a rare moment of oppositional television in its representation of menarche. The episode illustrates the adolescent's fear, her embarrassment, and the parents' awkward desire to reframe a culturally devalued event into a positive transition toward adulthood. There is a moment of praise of menstruation that almost slips by the unobservant viewer: When Darlene says she'll probably start "throwing like a girl now," Roseanne says proudly, "Yeah you are! And now that you've got your period, you're going to be throwing a lot farther, too."

Roseanne may not be aware of it (and ABC executives are almost certainly not aware), but she has just provided a lesson to Darlene in existentialist feminism. Following Beauvoir, one is not born a woman, one becomes a woman. And one does so by *choosing* one's own path of existence, for menstruation is not the essence of femininity.

> In a sexually equalitarian society, woman would regard menstruation simply as her special way of reaching adult life; the human body in both men and women has other and more disagreeable needs to be taken care of, but they are easily adjusted to because, being common to all, they do not represent blemishes for anyone; the menses inspire horror in the adolescent girl because they throw her into an inferior and defective category. This sense of being declassed will weigh heavily upon her. She would retain her pride in her bleeding body if she did not lose her pride in being human. (Beauvoir, 1952: 354)

In telling Darlene she can choose the kind of woman she wants to be, Roseanne tries to help her daughter retain her pride in herself.

Only Women Bleed

In all of these television references to menarche, we see a recurring theme of difference between women and men. Menstruation is the biological marker of difference, and the parent-child interaction illustrates the perceived social differences. The father who can comfortably discuss menstruation with his daughter is rare, and it is a mother's role, and sometimes an older sister's supporting role, to facilitate the transition to womanhood. Counterexamples are rare.

At first glance, these programs may seem to be positive and powerful challenges to menstrual taboo. On one level, they certainly are: The mere acknowledgment of menarche and menstruation in prime-time television and mainstream cinema openly and sometimes bravely challenges the taboo of speaking of menstruation. One need not go very far back into television's history to recognize how groundbreaking it was for Darlene Connor and Rudy Huxtable to menstruate on the air. Those who remember early sitcoms such as *Father Knows Best* know that neither Princess nor Kitten ever had a period. Even the Brady girls didn't menstruate, though themes of gender and adolescence dominated nearly every episode of *The Brady Bunch.*

The visibility of menstruation on-screen today is even more remarkable when one recognizes that the proportion of television characters who are female has changed very little over the years in spite of increasing numbers of women entering formerly male occupations, social roles, and political positions off-screen. Men on television continue to outnumber women two to one, and mature women are nearly invisible—almost nine out of ten female characters are under the age of 46 (Gerbner, 1998), suggesting we are unlikely to see frequent plot lines about menopause to parallel the menarche stories described here.[3] Portrayals of femininity and masculinity in film and television remain highly stereotypical, limited in scope, and nearly always represented as more different than alike, often as polar opposites. Male characters focus on work, while female characters concentrate on relationships; men are aggressive and independent, while women are passive and dependent; and so on (Signorelli, 1997; Wood, 1998). Representations of menstruation and menarche are nearly always used to reinforce that perceived dichotomy rather than challenge it.

But like menstruation in US culture, mass media present viewers with a paradox. Visual culture is simultaneously confirmatory and disruptive of ideology and stereotypes. A sign, such as menstruation, may appear to have a fixed or natural meaning, but only because it has so frequently been articulated as such. The inherent polysemy of media texts means that every text contains elements that allow readers to undermine the preferred meaning. Often these moments are fleeting, and nearly always they are disavowed in the narrative's conclusion, but these oppositional moments give feminist critics some hope. Perhaps one day, menstruation will become a fact of life for everyone, on-screen and off, rather than each woman's paradoxical secret shame and pride.

Notes

1. As noted in Chapter 1, my sampling of media representations is not systematic. I relied on memory and word-of-mouth to locate movies and television programs that featured scenes of menarche. I located four movies with such scenes: *My Girl, A Walk on the Moon, Ginger Snaps,* and the well-known opening scene from *Carrie.* I also recalled or heard about menarche episodes in the following TV shows: *Blossom, The Cosby Show, Roseanne, Something So Right, Cosby, 7th Heaven, ER, Everwood,* and *King of the Hill.* I do not claim that these are the only films or television programs that have addressed menarche or menstruation.

2. Historical explanations for the meaning of the slap vary from a punishment for pride at menstruation to a means of bringing the blood and color back to the cheeks to "I don't know, but my mother did it to me" (Culpepper, 1991).

3. I am aware of only two: *Golden Girls* ran an episode about the menopause of the character Blanche, not entirely out of place in a program in which the main characters were all women in late middle age or older; and *South Park* once featured a minor plot line in which one of the boy's mothers was saddened that her Aunt Flo would no longer visit. There are quite likely more, but as menopause is not the focus of my research, I have made no effort to track them.

4

Pills, Profits, PMS, and PMDD

UNLIKE MENSTRUATION, IT'S NOT DIFFICULT TO FIND REFERENCES to PMS in popular culture. In addition to magazine articles and television talk shows about PMS remedies and prevention, we can find coffee mugs, t-shirts, and buttons portraying women's cycles as a source of humor. My own collection includes a button that proclaims, "It's not PMS, I'm always bitchy" and a coffee mug that warns, "Beware! I'm armed and have premenstrual tension," among others. Men label women and women label themselves and each other as "PMS-ing" in casual conversation.

PMS isn't just a joke, however; in the early 1980s, before the discovery of AIDS, PMS was poised to become "the disease of the 80s." The explosion of self-help books and magazine articles about PMS in that decade seemed to erase all doubts about the frequency and commonality of PMS. Twenty years later, PMS is again attracting media and medical attention. In the summer of 2000, the Food and Drug and Administration (FDA) approved a new drug called Sarafem for treatment of premenstrual dysphoric disorder. Sarafem is a trademark owned by Eli Lilly for fluoxetine hydrochloride, the same active ingredient in Prozac, another trademark owned by the same company. Eli Lilly launched a multimillion-dollar ad campaign, reportedly spending $17 million in a three-month period marketing Sarafem directly to consumers and more than $16 million over six months promoting the drug to doctors and in scientific journals (Vedantam, 2001). With its portrayal of severe PMS as a mental illness with a prescription drug its only cure, this Sarafem marketing campaign is part of a larger trend of the corporate construction of disease.

What Is PMS?

The first to identify and document premenstrual symptoms as a clinical entity was Dr. Robert Frank in 1931. *Premenstrual tension,* as it was called then, included physiological symptoms such as headache, backache, abdominal pain, breast fullness and discomfort, weight gain, abdominal distension, fatigue, and nausea, and/or emotional symptoms such as depression, problems concentrating, nervousness, irritability, restlessness, and tension, all relieved with the onset of menstrual bleeding (Rodin, 1992). Definitions and symptoms of PMS vary by study, woman, and even across cycles within the same woman. The most commonly reported symptoms have been reported to occur at any time during the menstrual cycle (Abplanalp, 1983; Bancroft, 1995; Gurevich, 1995). More than 150 symptoms of premenstrual syndrome have been identified (Table 4.1). Estimates of the prevalence of premenstrual syndrome vary from 5 percent to 97 percent of women. More than 327 treatments have been proposed; so far, empirical evidence supports effectiveness of only two—exercise (Gurevich, 1995) and calcium carbonate tablets (Daw, 2002).

The newer term, *premenstrual syndrome,* is believed to have been coined in 1953 by British doctor Katharina Dalton (Johnson, 1987; Rodin, 1992). The apparent intent of the PMS concept was to separate problems associated with menstruation from those associated with other points in the cycle and to emphasize the variety of physiological changes associated with the ovarian cycle, most of which are not problematic (Bancroft, 1995). In fact, women all over the world have arguably experienced for centuries such "symptoms" as fluid retention, fatigue, bursts of energy, or irritability in advance of menstruation, but only in contemporary Western societies do these experiences constitute a syndrome. The labeling of premenstrual changes as *syndrome* bolsters perceptions of their seriousness and marks the phenomenon as in need of medical attention (Chrisler and Caplan, 2002).

Dalton's use of the term, and its use by the general population in the United States, has become less precise and more inclusive over time.[1] Dalton's current definition of PMS now incorporates "any pathological variation in hormone levels" and may include up to 17 days of each cycle (Rodin, 1992). The concept has become so elastic that it can apply to any woman, for as much as half of her menstrual cycle (Chrisler and Caplan, 2002). However, there is no evidence of a hormonal basis for PMS; the hormonal cycles of women who claim

Table 4.1 Common Symptoms of Premenstrual Syndrome

Affective	Autonomic
Sadness	Nausea
Anxiety	Diarrhea
Anger	Palpitations
Irritability	Sweating
Labile mood	
	Central Nervous System
Cognitive	Clumsiness
Decreased concentration	Seizures
Indecision	Dizziness
Paranoia	Vertigo
"Rejection sensitive"	Numbness/tingling
Suicidal ideation	
	Fluid/Electrolyte
Pain	Bloating
Headache	Weight gain
Breast tenderness	Diminished urine output
Joint and muscle pain	Edema
Behavioral	Dermatological
Decreased motivation	Acne
Poor impulse control	Greasy hair
Decreased efficiency	Dry hair
Social isolation	
Autonomic Nervous System	
Insomnia	
Hypersomnia	
Anorexia	
Craving for certain foods	
Fatigue	
Lethargy	
Agitation	
Libido change	

Source: Adapted from T. M. Johnson (1987). "Premenstrual Syndrome as a Western Culture-Specific Disorder." *Culture, Medicine and Psychiatry* 11: 337–356. Used with kind permission of Springer Science and Business Media.

to suffer from PMS are indistinguishable from those of other women (Bancroft, 1995). There is no blood test or other diagnostic test that can differentiate among PMS, PMDD, and normal ovulation (Young, 2001).

Though PMS has now been a subject of scientific research in Western nations for more than seventy years, there is still no consensus on the definition of premenstrual syndrome, nor its etiology or treatment. Many also debate its utility as a construct, saying it has little use diagnostically or therapeutically (Gurevich, 1995). Although many women believe they have PMS, when they seek medical treat-

ment, they often find that they don't fit the criteria for medical diagnosis and are frequently disappointed (Bancroft, 1995). Women who
visit PMS clinics do so most frequently for depression. Many of
these women are chronically depressed, and others are struggling
with major life problems (Bancroft, 1995) or suffering from other mood
or anxiety disorders (Bailey and Cohen, 1999). Some researchers have
found that women reporting severe PMS are more likely to be mar-
ried and working at home caring for small children (Gallant and
Hamilton, 1988).

Feminist critiques of the construct of PMS go back at least
twenty years: Andrea Eagan's analysis, "The Selling of Premenstrual
Syndrome: Who Profits from Making PMS 'the Disease of the
1980s'?" was originally published in *Ms.* in October 1983 (Eagan,
1985).[2] Feminists questioned the medicalization of another aspect of
female cycles and the potential consequences of its implication that
most women are "ill" once a month and require medical treatment to
cope with their "disease" (Rittenhouse, 1991). British researcher
Sophie Laws notes that many women do experience cyclical changes
corresponding to their menstrual cycles; this is not disputed. However, this does not mean that such changes are abnormal or a syndrome or markers of disease which require medical treatment.
Women, rather than the medical industry, need to define these changes
(Gurevich, 1995; Laws, 1985). As Gallant and Hamilton (1988) point
out, it is not necessary to pathologize menstruation to acknowledge
that it affects women's health and well-being.

Feminist criticism of PMS also includes broad criticism of the
increasing medicalization of women's lives. Medicalization has been
defined by sociologists as a process in which nonmedical problems
become defined and treated as medical problems and often taken out
of context, allowing the focus to shift from social and environmental
concerns to individual problems (Mintzes, 2002). Numerous feminist
critics, such as Emily Martin (1987), Barbara Ehrenreich and Deirdre
English (1978), and others, have noted how uniquely female biological processes, most notably childbirth, have come to be treated as
diseases as the modern medical profession evolved. Some critics
assert that the medicalization of ordinary life has shifted to overt disease mongering by pharmaceutical companies (Moynihan, Heath,
and Henry, 2002; Moynihan and Cassels, 2005).

As so-called lifestyle drugs—remedies "that may one day free the
world from the scourge of toenail fungus, obesity, baldness, face wrin-
kles and impotence" (Silverstein, 1999: 1)—increase in popularity and

profitability, everyone's lives are becoming increasingly medicalized. This process of commodification of medicine in the late twentieth and early twenty-first century is transforming our cultural definitions of health and illness: Market imperatives will continue to change not only how we perceive drugs as commodities, but also the "symbolic and discursive meaning of disease" (Tracy, 2004: 17). Or as Moynihan, Heath, and Henry (2002) more succinctly phrase it, "[t]he social construction of illness is being replaced by the corporate construction of disease" (p. 886). Drug companies regularly fund clinical research of treatments and sponsor meetings in which diseases are defined (Avorn, 2004; Healy, 2000, 2004; Moynihan, Heath, and Henry, 2002). It is common for clinical trials that do not produce favorable results for the treatment tested to be withheld and for successful trials to be reported several times (Healy, 2000).

Industry publications are not subtle about this agenda; a brief article in *Medical Marketing and Media* describes "The Art of Branding a Condition" (Parry, 2003). In advertising lingo, *branding* refers to creating a unique identity for a product that makes it memorable, desirable, and distinct from its competitors. Branding a condition means "defin[ing] a particular condition in the minds of physicians and patients [so that] you can also predicate the best treatment for that condition" (Parry, 2003: 43). Eli Lilly's work with PMDD and Sarafem, discussed in more detail below, is cited in Parry's article as a particularly stellar example of this process. It is not yet clear if direct-to-consumer advertising of prescription drugs has caused unnecessary labeling of patients or risky prescription practices, but it is clear that drug sales have increased since the FDA lifted the ban on direct-to-consumer drug ads (Moynihan and Cassels, 2005). It is unlikely coincidental that the best-selling drugs of modern medicine are not those that treat diseases, but drugs that manage conditions that have come to be seen as risks, such as hypertensives (for high blood pressure) and statins (for high cholesterol), and in the view of some critics, antidepressants (Healy, 2000).

PMS provides a striking example of how ordinary experience, particularly of women, can be easily medicalized. Feminist critics have observed that nearly every trait associated with cyclical changes is a negative trait or a perceived loss of ability, such as lack of concentration, decreased efficiency, decreased interest in social activity, lowered judgment, and so on. Martin (1988) asks if these perceived losses are accompanied by gains in complementary areas, such as ability to free-associate or to relax more deeply. She notes that many women report heightened emotional responsiveness, creativity, and physical sensuality during the days just before their menstrual flow, but these traits are seldom associated with PMS or given the opportunity to flourish premenstrually (Martin, 1988). Such alternative interpretations of premenstrual changes do not regard it as a "syndrome" and do not give it a distinct label.

In many ways similar to the prevalence of hysteria among middle- and upper-class women in the nineteenth century, PMS provides an excuse for women's anger and other emotions not consistent with ideals of femininity, which come from woman's passive construction as Other and as a vehicle for male confirmation (Beauvoir, 1952). A woman who is moody or angry, whether at her partner or her situation, is not focused on fulfilling her role as wife, mother, and helpmate. PMS thus becomes a survival tool for women in a culture that allows these feelings no other outlet (Gurevich, 1995; Martin, 1987). Medical anthropologist Thomas M. Johnson (1987) asks why PMS appears only in Western industrial cultures, only in the latter half of the twentieth century, when premenstrual symptoms have been reported in numerous societies for centuries: "PMS involves bizarre behavior which is recognized, defined, and treated as a specific syndrome only by biomedical healers in Western, industrialized cultures, and can only be understood in this specific cultural context" (Johnson, 1987: 347).

Johnson speculates that PMS serves as a means for modern Western women to respond to the role conflicts of our era (mother and employee), by "symbolically denying the possibility of each: in menstruating, one is potentially fertile but obviously not pregnant; in having incapacitating symptomatology, one is exempted from normal work role expectations" (Johnson, 1987: 349). That is, PMS functions as a "safety valve" that allows women to reject, if only temporarily, the competing demands of paid work and motherhood.

To put it another way, PMS becomes a socially approved way for a woman to temporarily escape her responsibilities. Johnson seemed to be referring to the often tedious demands of housework and child-care—and they're certainly among the responsibilities cited in the numerous anecdotal tales in popular books like Katharina Dalton's works on PMS—but Emily Martin's anthropological research and perceptive analysis (1987) adds keeping one's negative emotions suppressed to the list of duties from which PMS exempts women. This is also referenced, although not explicitly as a duty, in Dalton's case studies and examples:

"Pity those around me when the least things upset me, I hate everyone, shouting and picking quarrels, and the whole world gets on my nerves and I can only look at it with a jaundiced eye." (quoted in Dalton, 1978: 42)

"Last Saturday I deliberately smashed all the dishes after clearing the table. I started menstruating in the evening. My general practitioner puts it down to my Irish temper. I get so depressed, hateful, horrid, tired, I stay in bed, shout and I could go on and on like this. It is my husband who asked me to write [you] for help." (quoted in Dalton, 1978: 44)

"My husband has urged me to write; our marriage is breaking up, our children are suffering and after five years of trouble my poor husband can take no more." (quoted in Dalton, 1978: 100)

A woman's anger (at her spouse, her children, or her situation) is permitted only when it can be attributed to PMS—and thus easily dismissed or treated. Martin wonders why, if during the premenstrual phase women purportedly have less control over their emotions, rage is what surfaces.

Perhaps that rage is lurking just below the veneer of femininity, *all the time.* The treatments proposed in popular works such as Dalton's book typically attribute the rage to the menstrual cycle, rather than searching for underlying sources of anger that emerge premenstrually. Such a search would require a thorough examination and acknowledgment of social, political, and economic inequities documented by feminists and a widespread commitment to social change. It's easier to blame—and treat—hormones for women's anger or moodiness.

Some women's health activists promote an alternative understanding of PMS consistent with Martin's phenomenology of menstruation. For example, Alexandra Pope maintains that PMS is an amplification of a woman's ongoing social or health problems. She writes that "the menstrual cycle isn't *causing* the problem[,] it's *revealing* it through increased psychological and physical sensitivity" (Pope, 2001: 81, emphasis in original). Similarly, Christiane Northrup sees PMS as a time of heightened sensitivity, "*when women are most in tune with their inner knowing and with what isn't working in their lives*" (1998: 107, emphasis in original). Northrup encourages women to see this heightened sensitivity as a gift and to accommodate the body's need to slow down just before and during menstruation. Both of these writers retain the focus on the life and personal choices of the individual.

Research indicates that women with symptoms of PMS (and PMDD) are far more likely than other women to be in difficult or stressful life situations, such as being battered at home or mistreated at work, and thus have good reason for anger. Putting these women on antidepressants does nothing to alleviate the situations causing their pain and labels their problems as individual and psychological, rather than social and material (Caplan, 2001; Chrisler and Caplan, 2002).

Selling remedies to individuals is indubitably more profitable than working to change society. Blaming social problems on women's menstrual cycles or even their own character flaws supports the ongoing social construction of woman as Other that Beauvoir described. If a problem affects only women, rather than "people," it is easier still to see it as individual and psychological, rather than societal. The FDA Advisory Committee that approved Sarafem recommended prescribing the drug for PMDD only when symptoms were severe enough "to interfere with functioning at work or school, or with social activities and relationships" (Food and Drug Administration, 2000)—or in other words, when they started to bother someone other than the premenstrual woman.

In his best-selling 1993 book, *Listening to Prozac,* Peter Kramer coined the term *cosmetic psychopharmacology* to describe the use of medication to alter personality traits rather than to treat illness or repair brain damage. Kramer's analysis does not address cosmetic psychopharmacology as a gendered issue, but the long history of medicalization of women's lives suggests that the use of Sarafem to treat PMDD appears to be another excellent example of this phenomenon. Even the drug's name is evocative of its intended personality transformation: *Sarafem* is homonymous with *seraphim,* the highest ranked of the medieval Christian hierarchy of angels. Sarafem is designed to make women more angelic.

Development of PMDD

The American Psychiatric Association (APA), however, did not accept the feminist proposition that cyclic changes are normal, rather than pathological. In 1985, a new diagnosis, Premenstrual Dysphoric Disorder (PDD), was proposed for inclusion in the upcoming revision of the APA's *Diagnostic and Statistical Manual of Mental Disorders,* known informally as the *DSM* (Caplan, 1995; Figert, 1996).[3] The *DSM* is a widely used system for classifying and diagnosing mental illness. It is used not only by clinicians, researchers, and students, but by the judicial system to assess parents involved in custody disputes and to judge the mental capacity of accused criminals; by school psychologists to make referrals for medication; by Medicaid and Social Security to determine funding; by foundations and government agencies to make decisions about grant support; by health-care providers and insurance companies to determine reimbursement for psychotherapy, hospitalization, sex reassignment surgery, and drugs. It is also used by prisons, welfare agencies, and the US military. The current edition, *DSM-IV* published in 1994, includes more than 300 disorders and 400 distinct diagnoses (Levine, 2001).

The work group to revise *DSM-III* first met in the summer of 1983, and by November of 1984, they had established twenty-six specialized advisory committees to assist in the evaluation of specific disorders. Dr. Robert Spitzer of the New York Psychiatric Institute chaired the work group and thus also chaired all twenty-six advisory committees. One of these was the "Premenstrual Advisory Committee" (Figert, 1996). The advisory committees were charged with the task of assessing whether each proposed new category met the *DSM-III* definition of mental disorder and whether there was a compelling research or clinical need for the new diagnosis (Figert, 1996). Debate and controversy over making PMS a psychiatric disorder began almost immediately.

Teresa Bernardez, then Chair of the APA Committee on Women, presented the Committee's objections to the advisory group, offering two main critiques: First, the diagnosis had the potential to stigmatize all women, and second, scientific data were inadequate to support inclusion in the *DSM-III-R*. The Advisory Committee voted for inclusion of the newly renamed *periluteal phase dysphoric disorder* (PLPDD) anyway (Figert, 1996). The Committee on Women's two concerns were raised repeatedly by many parties during the years of debate that followed.

The Committee on Women continued to protest the inclusion of a premenstrual diagnosis in *DSM-III-R* with memos, letters, radio and television appearances, and participation in meetings (Figert, 1996). Spitzer unsuccessfully tried to appease the Committee on Women by adding disclaimers in the text. Eventually, more than twenty professional organizations of psychiatrists and psychologists spoke out publicly against the inclusion of a premenstrual diagnosis in the *DSM-III-R* (Figert, 1996). Gynecologists also objected, arguing that PMS was a physiological or biological disorder and that they were better suited to diagnose and treat it. It already had a classification in the equivalent medical reference work, *International Classification of Diseases* (ICD-9-CM), where it was coded number 625.40, Premenstrual Tension Syndrome (Figert, 1996).

After months of meetings and debate, the APA's Board of Directors voted in the summer of 1986 to place the PMS-related diagnosis PLPDD in the appendix of the *DSM-III-R* (Caplan, 1995; Figert, 1996). The APA president that year, Robert Pasnau, remarked that although there was insufficient scientific evidence in favor, PLPDD was "of sufficient clinical importance to justify publishing [it] in the appendix to the manual for research and educational purposes" (quoted in Figert, 1996: 46). The final draft of the *DSM-III-R* was accepted and approved by the board that December, with the premenstrual diagnosis in the appendix under yet another new name, *late luteal phase dysphoric disorder* (LLPDD), with the code number 307.90: Other and Unspecified Symptoms or Syndromes, Not Elsewhere Classified. Issuance of a code number was debated almost as hotly as the diagnosis itself, because a code number legitimates a diagnosis for insurance, legal, and diagnostic purposes (Figert, 1996). When the *DSM-III-R* appeared in print in May 1987, there was a reference to LLPDD in the main text as well as in the appendix, and the appendix instructed researchers and clinicians to assign the code number 300.90, Unspecified Mental Disorder, Late Luteal Phase Dysphoric Disorder (Figert, 1996). (See Table 4.2 for criteria included for this diagnosis.)

Label-changing is a common feature of *DSM* procedures, and the permutations of the name for this diagnosis were no exception (Caplan, 1995; Figert, 1996). The initially proposed term, *premenstrual dysphoric disorder* (PDD), literally means "bad mood before menstruation." APA leaders debated whether this label would stigmatize women, and the name was briefly changed to periluteal phase dysphoric disorder to avoid, according to Spitzer, the stigma of "the curse" and to recognize that some women who do not menstruate may experience the disorder (Figert, 1996). The later label of late luteal phase dysphoric disorder gave the appearance of a greater scientific precision than the data warranted by identifying a highly specific few days late in the luteal phase of the cycle (Figert, 1996). It also obscured the menstrual connection to those unfamiliar with scientific language, which Caplan (1995) speculates made it harder for outsiders to examine or question the diagnosis. The diagnosis was returned to its original name, *premenstrual dysphoric disorder*, albeit with a slightly different acronym (PMDD) for the publication of *DSM-IV* in 1994 (Caplan, 1995; Figert, 1996).[4] Figert (1996) suggests

Table 4.2 *DSM-III-R* **Criteria for LLPDD**

A. In most menstrual cycles during the past year, symptoms in B occurred during the last week of the luteal phase and remitted within a few days after the onset of the follicular phase. In menstruating females, these phases correspond to the week before, and a few days after, the onset of menses. (In nonmenstruating females who have had a hysterectomy, the timing of the luteal and follicular phases may require measurement of circulating reproductive hormones.)

B. At least five of the following symptoms have been present for most of the time during each symptomatic late luteal phase, at least one of the symptoms being 1, 2, 3, or 4.

   1. Marked affective lability, e.g., feeling suddenly sad, tearful, irritable, or angry
   2. Persistent and marked anger or
   3. Marked anxiety, tension, feeling of being "keyed up" or "on edge"
   4. Markedly depressed mood, feelings of hopelessness, or self-deprecating thoughts
   5. Decreased interest in usual activities, e.g., work, school, friends, hobbies
   6. Easy fatigability, or marked lack of energy
   7. Subjective sense of difficulty in concentrating
   8. Marked change in appetite, overeating, or specific food cravings
   9. Hypersomnia or insomnia
  10. A subjective sense of being overwhelmed or out of control
  11. Other physical symptoms, such as breast tenderness or swelling, headaches, joint or muscle pain, "bloating," or weight gain

C. The disturbance seriously interferes with work or with usual social activities or relationships with others.

D. The disturbance is not merely an exacerbation of the symptoms of another disorder, such as Major Depressive Disorder, Panic Disorder, Dysthymia, or a Personality Disorder (although it may be superimposed on any of these disorders).

E. Criteria A, B, C and D must be confirmed by prospective daily self-ratings during at least two symptomatic cycles. (The diagnosis may be made provisionally prior to this confirmation.)

Source: Used with permission from American Psychiatric Association, *Diagnostic and Statistical Manual of Mental Disorders,* 3rd ed. rev. (Washington, D.C.: American Psychiatric Association, 1987).

this was done to make the diagnosis more accessible to *DSM-IV* users. Apparently, few knew what "late luteal phase" meant, but everyone understood "premenstrual." The new label also blurs the distinction between PMDD and ordinary PMS—arguably a marketing advantage but not a diagnostic one.

After publication of *DSM-III-R,* work began almost immediately on *DSM-IV* under the leadership of Allen Francis (Caplan, 1995). The APA tried to minimize controversy over this round of revisions and vowed explicitly that decisions about the manual would be based upon scientific data, not politics (Figert, 1996). Judith Gold, a clinician and PMS researcher, was appointed to chair the PMDD work group (Figert, 1996). Its task was to evaluate the research on premenstrual dysphoric disorder and decide whether it should retain its provisional listing in the appendix and the main text, be listed in the main text only, or be removed entirely (Caplan, 1995). Paula Caplan, a psychotherapist, professor, and very public opponent of including a premenstrual diagnosis in the earlier revision of *DSM,* was invited by Francis in 1988 to serve on the work group. Although involved in collaboration on numerous literature reviews and committee meetings, Caplan resigned from the work group two years later out of concern for the poor science, misrepresentations, and distortions of evidence by the *DSM* task forces (Caplan, 1995).

The work group continued its examination of the research without Caplan and continued to face vigorous public debate and opposition. Concerns were again raised about the risk of stigmatizing all women. Proponents of the diagnosis responded that only about 5 percent of all menstruating women would likely be eligible for this diagnosis; opponents of the diagnosis responded that labeling half a million women in the United States mentally ill is not insignificant (Caplan, 1995). Sally Severino's analysis of menstrual cycle data from 1,089 women seeking treatment for PMS showed greater variability in who might be diagnosed: Because there is not a reliable method for making the diagnosis, anywhere from 14 percent to 45 percent of the women in her sample could receive the new diagnosis (Span, 1993). At this point in the process, Severino withdrew from the committee. She later told medical journalist Ray Moynihan that putting PMDD in the manual was a political decision, not a scientific one (Moynihan and Cassels, 2005).

Caplan and her colleagues pointed out several dangerous implications of the fuzzy diagnostic criteria: (1) women feared losing their children in custody disputes if they were labeled mentally ill with PMDD; (2) employers might claim that a woman's premenstrual psychiatric disorder justified firing or not hiring her in the first place; (3) women could suffer severe side effects from antidepressants, so far the only proposed treatment for PMDD;[5] (4) physicians might miss painful or deteriorating physical problems, such as worsening sexually transmitted diseases or infections, by focusing on emotional symptoms that are secondary to the pain; and (5) women might experience increased anxiety or depression from being labeled mentally ill (Caplan, 1995).

Issues raised by others included (6) the potential for misdiagnosis among women who may suffer from more severe mental disorders, (7) whether PMDD is really distinct from an underlying depressive disorder (Figert, 1996), and (8) the potential of iatrogenic effects of the diagnosis—in other words, the risk that some patients may experience more intense symptoms as a result of being diagnosed with PMDD (Gallant and Hamilton, 1988). Given that women currently experience depression at twice the rate of men, distinguishing PMDD from an underlying or more severe depressive condition is a nontrivial concern (Sanacore, 2003; Young, Campbell, and Harper, 2002). Critics have pointed to the difficulty of establishing a differential diagnosis using the proposed criteria; in other words, the criteria used to identify PMDD can not distinguish women with the disorder from women without it—or from men, as diary research has shown (Gallant and Hamilton, 1988; see Table 4.3). Some researchers have in fact found greater mood fluctuation over the days of the week than over the course of the menstrual cycle, with women reporting no greater mood fluctuation than men (McFarlane, Martin, and Williams, 1988).

Another criticism of the diagnosis was its reliance on retrospective self-report, requiring no external validation. It has been well-documented that women's reports of PMS symptoms and their severity are worse in retrospective reports than when reported concurrently (Caplan, 1995; Gallant et al., 1992a, 1992b; McFarlane, Martin, and Williams, 1988). In addition, there were no empirically proven medical treatments for the proposed disorder (Caplan, 1995), although some doctors were experimenting with the new class of antidepressants

Table 4.3 Comparison of Diagnostic Criteria for LLPDD, Depression, and Dysthymia

Proposed LLPDD Disorder	Major Depression	Dysthymic Disorder
Affective lability, e.g., feeling suddenly sad, tearful, irritable, or angry	B	A
Persistent anger or irritability	C	A
Tension, feeling of being "keyed up"	C	C
Depressed mood, self-deprecation	A	A
Decreased interest in activities	A	A
Easy fatigability, lack of energy	A	A
Subjective sense of difficulty concentrating	A	A
Change in appetite, overeating, or food cravings	A	C
Hypersomnia or insomnia	A	A
Serious interference with work or with usual social activities or relationships		A

Source: S. J. Gallant and J. A. Hamilton. (1988). "On a Premenstrual Psychiatric Diagnosis: What's in a Name? *Professional Psychology: Research and Practice* 19, no. 3: 271–278. Reprinted with permission. © 1988 by the American Psychological Association.
Notes: A = same or very similar; B = related, less similar; C = different.

known as selective serotonin reuptake inhibitors (SSRIs), such as Prozac and Zoloft. These antidepressants are the APA-recommended treatment for PMDD, although they are no more effective than placebos for premenstrual symptoms. As noted above, exercise and calcium tablets both have been shown to have greater effectiveness than either drug (Daw, 2002; Gurevich, 1995).

Eventually, in the summer of 1993, the work group and the Board of Directors approved the inclusion of PMDD, with only minor changes in the existing criteria in the *DSM-IV* in 1994 (Figert, 1996). Although PMDD remains in an appendix of the *DSM* and thus is technically a research category rather than a diagnostic label, its presence in the volume with a code number has made it functionally an official diagnosis. A woman can be diagnosed with PMDD when she experiences at least five of the eleven symptoms, with one being either feelings of sadness, hopelessness, or self-deprecation; feelings of tension, anxiety, or being on edge; sudden mood changes or sadness; or persistent anger or irritability during the week before menstruation begins (American Psychiatric Association, 1994). That is, at least one of her symptoms must be emotional. There is still no known etiology for PMDD and no empirical evidence that it exists.

The Selling of Sarafem

With PMDD firmly established in the *DSM-IV*, the markets were now ripe for selling the cure. The drug industry is the most profitable industry in the United States, with Americans spending $117 billion annually ("Drug Industry Most Profitable in U.S.," 2001; Moynihan and Cassels, 2005).

Clinical tests of fluoxetine hydrochloride for PMDD, better known by its patented trade name, Prozac, were already under way when the *DSM-IV* was published, and doctors had been prescribing it off-label for severe emotional symptoms of PMS almost since its release ("FDA Panel Recommends Fluoxetine for PMDD," 1999). On July 6, 2000, the FDA approved fluoxetine, in the form of the new drug Sarafem, as the first drug treatment for PMDD (Food and Drug Administration, 2000). This type of approval is not uncommon: Two-thirds of drugs approved in the last twelve years were reformulations of existing drugs. The price of newly approved drugs are frequently nearly twice the cost of older versions (Petersen, 2002). By the end of 2000, with Sarafem on the market for less than six months, $8 million worth of prescriptions had been sold (Gadsby, 2001). Doctors had written more than 202,000 prescriptions for Sarafem by the following spring (Matthews, 2001).

Many responded cynically to the FDA approval, noting that the patent on Prozac was due to expire in 2001 and Eli Lilly, its manufacturer, would soon see a significant decrease in profits as generic fluoxetine became available. By the mid-1990s, Prozac accounted for more than 10 percent of Eli Lilly's annual sales (Breggin and Breggin, 1994). Analysts estimated that Eli Lilly would see a decline from more than $2.5 billion in 2000 to $625 million in 2003, due to the expiration of Prozac's patent. Because Eli Lilly is the exclusive patent holder on Sarafem, they can set the price (Maher, 2001; Matthews, 2001). The patent does not permit doctors or pharmacists to substitute generic fluoxetine for patients with PMDD ("Marketing Madness: Drugs," 2001), as the FDA "Orange Book" (*Approved Drug Products with Therapeutic Equivalence Evaluations*) lists Sarafem as having no generic equivalent ("Generic Substitution Issues," 2001). Creating a separate trademark would also allow Eli Lilly to escape some of the Prozac backlash and associated bad press, and might lessen the stigma associated with antidepressants (Spartos, 2000).

Sarafem is chemically identical to Prozac; its only difference is the color of the gelatin capsules. Sarafem comes in pink or pink and lavender, while Prozac is green and white, leading more than one critic to label the new drug "Prozac in drag" (Kramer, 2000). Eli Lilly defended the development of this "new" drug specifically for PMDD treatment with the assertion that "women told us they wanted treatment that would differentiate PMDD from depression" (Spartos, 2000). Given that antidepressant drugs are currently the top-selling prescription category in the United States, totaling $10.4 billion in 2000—a 21 percent increase from the previous year (Gadsby, 2001)—it would seem that any perceived stigma attached to taking antidepressants has begun to fade on its own.

Escaping the Prozac backlash may not be so simple. A number of critics, many of whom are psychiatrists, have publicly pointed out dangers of fluoxetine. Peter and Ginger Breggin have co-authored *Talking Back to Prozac: What Doctors Won't Tell You about Today's Most Controversial Drug* (1994), in which they compare Prozac to amphetamines in function and potential dangers. In 2000, Joseph Glenmullen published *Prozac Backlash: Overcoming the Dangers of Prozac, Zoloft, Paxil, and Other Antidepressants With Safe, Effective Alternatives,* in which he recommends psychotherapy and St. John's wort over prescription drugs. In 2001, Bruce Levine published *Commonsense Rebellion: Debunking Psychiatry, Confronting Society,* in which he takes on not only Prozac and other psychotropic drugs, but the entire *DSM* and most current trends in psychiatric treatment. Most recently, David Healy wrote *Let Them Eat Prozac* (2004), a thorough examination of the relationship between the pharmaceutical industry and depression. Healy details the lawsuits and trials Eli Lilly has faced (and continues to face), including his own role as an expert witness and the professional consequences he has experienced for his criticism.

Some mental health professionals have accused these writers of seeking media attention and self-aggrandizement, but their serious questions about the safety of Prozac deserve attention. Levine (2001) claims that more than 40,000 reports of adverse effects have been received by the FDA, which estimates that only 1 percent of serious side effects for any drug are ever reported to them. Reported adverse effects of Prozac include the development of tics and other involuntary movements as well as a Parkinson's-like condition, diminished effectiveness of the drug over time, and withdrawal symptoms (Glenmullen, 2000). Prozac has also been charged with producing violent or suicidal reactions and has been named in more than 200 lawsuits against Eli Lilly (Huffington, 2000). Breggin has served as an expert witness in numerous product liability suits against drug companies, testifying on behalf of plaintiffs that these drugs can cause disinhibition and mania that may have led to criminal acts (Breggin, 2002).

A well-known side effect of fluoxetine, and of most SSRIs, is sexual dysfunction. At least 60 percent of users of SSRIs experience some form of sexual difficulty; most frequently reported are loss of libido and inability to achieve orgasm (Glenmullen, 2000). Although these effects are noted in the FDA labeling of Sarafem for patients, there's more than a little irony in a prescription intended to help women with relationship difficulties caused by premenstrual symptoms having the effect of diminishing their interest in and ability to enjoy physical intimacy with their partners.

A recent ABC News poll found that 72 percent of patients using antidepressants believed that long-term studies have been conducted. They are wrong; FDA approval requires clinical tests of only six to twelve weeks, and long-term effects of continuous use of Prozac are unknown (Langer, 2000; Newman, 2000). Eli Lilly markets Prozac as relatively free of side effects, but advertisements for Sarafem list several side effects, such as upset stomach, tiredness, nervousness, and difficulty concentrating, along with the claim that "side effects are usually mild and tend to go away within a few weeks." For some women, the treatment may be worse than the disease, as all of these side effects of Sarafem appear on lists of PMS symptoms.

Some critics of the separation of Sarafem and Prozac point out that many women prescribed Sarafem may not be aware that it is the same drug and would otherwise choose not to take a mind-altering drug.[6] Others may already be taking another antidepressant and could be at risk for severe side effects or complications by inadvertently taking two (Caplan, 2001). In addition, fluoxetine is no more effective for relief of premenstrual mood changes than other widely prescribed antidepressants, such as sertraline (Zoloft), fluvoxamine (Luvox), and paroxetine (Paxil) (Kramer, 2000). Furthermore, meta-analysis of drug trials submitted to the FDA indicates that the difference in effectiveness between most of these antidepressant drugs and placebos is slight (Kirsch et al., 2002).

Another concern of Sarafem's critics is the possibility for misdiagnosis. Many symptoms of PMDD are easily confused with depression or thyroid disease (Maher, 2001). The average interview for mental illness by a nonspecialist is about three minutes, and due to changes in the health-care system and the direct-to-consumer marketing of Sarafem, Sarafem is likely to be prescribed largely by nonpsychiatrists (Clements, 2001).

Prescription by family practice physicians and gynecologists may well have been part of its design, although with the exception of depression, physicians (other than psychiatrists) rarely prescribe drugs for other *DSM* diagnoses. Robert Spitzer, one of the initial leaders of the APA's move to include a premenstrual diagnosis in the *DSM*, is also the lead developer of a biometric questionnaire, PrimeMD, that can be used by family practice doctors and other physicians to diagnose PMDD or other depressive illnesses and prescribe appropriate psychotropic drugs. The questionnaire relies on criteria from the DSM and is designed to be completed by the patient alone and then assessed quickly by the physician (Spitzer et al., n.d.).

The Sarafem Ad Campaign: "Think Again"

The direct-to-consumer ad campaign for Sarafem promotes what is essentially cosmetic psychopharmacology for women with premenstrual symptoms. The ad campaign's first television ad featured video images of a woman struggling with a shopping cart, while a voice-over read a list of symptoms: "irritability . . . mood swings . . . bloating.

. . . Think it's PMS? It could be PMDD." The FDA's Division of Drug Marketing, Advertising, and Communications requested that Eli Lilly remove this ad from circulation, objecting to the ad's failure to completely define PMDD and to distinguish it from PMS. The FDA's warning letter said the ad "trivializes the seriousness of PMDD" (Stockbridge, 2000). The ad was withdrawn, and Eli Lilly was not fined or sanctioned (Moynihan and Cassels, 2005).

The ad that replaced it trivializes women instead. The most prominent linguistic component of this ad campaign, in television and in print, is the slogan, "Think it's PMS? Think again." The clear presumption of this phrase is that women are wrong and should consult experts, because their own understanding of their physical and/or emotional symptoms cannot be trusted. As with other disease-mongering pharmaceutical campaigns, the ad strives to portray the condition as widespread and underdiagnosed.

In the new television commercial, three women are shown experiencing symptoms of PMDD: one is angry, shouting as her male partner attempts to mollify her; one is sad, sitting alone on a sofa and weeping; and one is bloated, shown unhappily trying on pants and frowning in the mirror of a department store dressing room. It is not clear, from the images or the voice-over, how these symptoms are different from ordinary PMS. The suggestion that women should take psychotropic drugs so that their pants will fit better is insulting and makes PMDD symptoms appear as trivial as the shopping cart struggles did. The tone of the ad invokes the specter of fear, encouraging women to see mood changes as pathological.

The ad further misrepresents PMDD in labeling it "a distinct medical condition." As the APA has spent years asserting, PMDD is a *psychiatric diagnosis*. PMS was already an established medical diagnosis, as premenstrual tension syndrome, in the ICD in the category of "Other Disorders of the Female Genital Tract," in the chapter, "Genitourinary System Diseases." This fact was one of the reasons professional societies of gynecologists argued against inclusion of PMDD in the DSM.

The magazine ads also mislead women about the diagnosis. The fall 2001 print ads were accompanied by a tear-out card with a checklist of symptoms to take to one's doctor, with the bold-print instruction to "think about how you feel the week before your period." As noted above, research finds that premenstrual symptoms are much worse in retrospective recall than in concurrently kept records (Caplan, 1995; Gallant et al., 1992a). Current *DSM-IV* guidelines recommend that a diagnosis of PMDD be made on the basis of carefully logged symptoms over a period of at least two consecutive cycles, not merely on the basis of recalled symptoms in a single office visit (American Psychiatric Association, 1994).

It is important to remember, however, that the function of advertisements is not to provide factual information about products but to attach social and emotional meanings to products. Sarafem, like ads for other antidepressant drugs, promises to restore women to their previous selves—their rightful roles as wives, mothers, and docile good girls (Preston and White, 2003). Ads are not required to provide accurate information about illness; while claims about the risks and benefits of drugs are (loosely) regulated, claims about the nature of diseases are not (Moynihan and Cassels, 2005). Sarafem's slogan, displayed next to the drug's name in magazine ads, Web pages, and television commercials, is "More like the woman you are." The clear implication here is that the premenstrual self is inauthentic; mood swings, irritability, and bloating aren't real feelings. Women must take psychotropic drugs to find their authentic selves (Kramer, 2000) and to suppress those unpleasant, unfeminine feelings that get in the way of their responsibilities. Medication can restore women to the "Eternal Feminine" that characterizes the absolute Other. The woman without PMS who is presupposed in these ads resembles the mythical Femininity Beauvoir identifies:

> If the definition provided for this concept is contradicted by the behavior of flesh-and-blood women, it is the latter who are wrong: we are told not that Femininity is a false entity, but that the women concerned are not feminine. (1952: 286)

What's Next?

Thomas M. Johnson (1987) published his analysis of PMS as a Western, culture-specific disorder nearly twenty years ago. Johnson notes that the term *culture-bound syndrome* is typically used by Western anthropologists to describe entities in other cultures and offers the following definition: "a constellation of symptoms categorized by a given culture as a disease; the etiology of which symbolizes core meanings and reflects preoccupations of the culture; and the diagnosis and treatment of which are dependent upon culture-specific technology and ideology" (Johnson, 1987: 338). Without denying the reality of physiological premenstrual symptoms, Johnson argued that premenstrual syndrome is best understood as a social and cultural phenomenon. Emily Martin's work amplifies Johnson's findings; she notes that the long list of symptoms of PMS is "not so much a list of traits that would be unfortunate in any circumstances but ones that happen to be unfortunate in the particular social and economic system, with the kind of work it generates, that we live in" (1988: 170).

It requires only a small leap to apply their analyses to PMDD. In his reflections on the societal impact of Prozac, Peter Kramer (1993) wondered if social coercion to take Prozac would emerge in US culture, analogous to the "free choice under pressure" felt by athletes to take steroids and fashion models to get breast implants. That is, no one holds a gun to the head of small-breasted fashion models, but only women with large breasts get the best modeling assignments and corresponding salaries (Kramer, 1993). If the current trends of drug prescription and pharmaceutical marketing continue, we may soon see the day when women between menarche and menopause experience a Hobson's Choice to take fluoxetine or other unneeded treatments.

At their biannual meeting in 2001, the Society for Menstrual Cycle Research (SMCR) passed a resolution calling upon the FDA to reconsider its approval of Sarafem and to enjoin Eli Lilly from airing or publishing advertisements for Sarafem until such reconsideration is completed. The society's primary claim against Sarafem is that there is no good empirical evidence that PMDD exists (Caplan, 2002). The SMCR, along with National Women's Health Network, the Boston Women's Health Book Collective, the Women's Health Initiative, and the Association for Women in Psychology, is part of the Coalition for Women's Health. The coalition held a briefing for members of Congress and their staffs in February 2002, sponsored by Rep. Louise Slaughter of New York, titled *Women, Drugs, and "Premenstrual Dysphoric Disorder": What Is Behind the Pathologizing of Mood Changes?*

Despite these protests and criticisms, it is unlikely that any changes will be made in FDA regulation, direct-to-consumer advertising, or the *DSM*. In May of 2002, the FDA announced approval of Zoloft, another SSRI, for the treatment of PMDD (Rowland, 2002). By the end of 2003, Paxil CR, yet another SSRI antidepressant, had joined the list of FDA-approved drugs for treatment of PMDD.

However, there is a slight glimmer of hope as of this writing. In early 2004, the Committee for Proprietary Medical Products, the European drug-regulating body (roughly equivalent to the FDA in the United States), ruled that PMDD is not a well-established disease entity and forced Eli Lilly to drop the alleged disorder from its listings for fluoxetine sales in Europe (Moynihan, 2004). Back in the United States, the FDA has yet to respond to demands for reconsideration.

Notes

1. In many cases, especially among younger women and men, the terms *PMS* and *PMS-ing* seem to stand in for menstruation in general.

2. It was reprinted with several other feminist critiques in 1985 in the collection *Seeing Red: The Politics of Premenstrual Tension.*

3. The controversy about the addition of a premenstrual diagnosis to the *DSM* has been thoroughly documented in Figert (1996) and Caplan (1995), and I have relied heavily on both to summarize how it happened.

4. For clarity and convenience, I will use the current term, *premenstrual dysphoric disorder,* or its new acronym, PMDD, from here forward.

5. Young women may be particularly vulnerable to side effects of fluoxetine, as it has recently been implicated in several suicides and suicide attempts (Healy, 2004).

6. To date, I have given three public presentations of my analysis of Sarafem and PMDD on university campuses, and each time, one or more audience members has told me of a physician recommending Sarafem for her PMS symptoms without telling her that it is equivalent to Prozac or that it is a psychotropic drug.

5

Manipulating Menstruation for Fun and Profit

THE YEAR 2003 BROUGHT ANOTHER DRAMATIC EXAMPLE OF THE increasing medicalization of women's lives as the FDA approved a new oral contraceptive designed to limit menstruation to four menstrual periods a year, rather than the typical thirteen most women experience. Seasonale, the new drug, is composed of levonorgestrel and ethinyl estradiol and is thus chemically very similar to oral contraceptives already available; the difference is that Seasonale is taken on a ninety-one-day regimen (eighty-four days of active pills plus seven days of placebos), whereas other oral contraceptives are based on a twenty-eight-day regimen (twenty-one days of active pills followed by seven days of placebos). With both types of pills, the woman will experience a withdrawal bleed during the seven days she takes the inactive pills.

Oral contraceptives, and other hormonal methods of birth control such as injections, vaginal inserts, and skin patches, work by suppressing ovulation. The increased quantity and consistency of hormone levels mimic pregnancy, so the pituitary gland does not trigger the hormonal chain of events that leads to ovulation. The abrupt decrease in hormonal levels when the pills are stopped (or the patch or insert removed) causes the endometrial lining to begin disintegration and expulsion. Because the uterine lining is thinner than it would be during a natural menstrual cycle, this withdrawal bleed is often much lighter in intensity and duration than a natural menstrual flow (Potter, 2001).

The introduction of Seasonale followed a surge of publicity for the idea of menstrual suppression. The ability of Seasonale and other oral contraceptives to inhibit menstruation was widely covered first in women's magazines and then in more generalized news outlets, such as the *New York Times, Newsweek,* National Public Radio (NPR), and numerous daily newspapers in cities large and small.

To Bleed or Not to Bleed?

The initial surge of publicity seemed to be triggered by Elsimar Coutinho's book, *Is Menstruation Obsolete?*, translated into English and published in the United States in 1999. (In the preface to this book, the original Portuguese title, *Menstruação: A Sangria Inútil,* is literally translated as "Menstruation, A Useless Bleeding" [Sheldon Segal in Coutinho, 1999].) Coutinho claims that suppressing menstruation through continuous use of birth control pills or by Depo-Provera injections is not only more natural than frequent menstruation but healthier and especially beneficial for women who suffer from anemia, PMS, or endometriosis. Elsimar Coutinho is a professor of gynecology and obstetrics at Federal University of Bahia School of Medicine in Brazil and researcher of contraception. He is widely known for his role in the development of the injectable hormonal contraceptive Depo-Provera. His argument for suppression or manipulation of menstruation is based in part on the assertion that regular, monthly menstruation is a recent evolutionary phenomenon brought about through social and cultural changes (Coutinho, 1999). Coutinho further asserts that menstruation generally does not benefit women and may in fact cause problems for many women. His primary examples of such problems are PMS and endometriosis.

Mainstream women's magazines in the United States, such as *Redbook, Glamour,* and others, have covered the issue of menstrual suppression, usually favorably and often without acknowledging Coutinho's book. These magazine articles frequently promote menstrual suppression, often with the threat of imminent cancer, as in *Glamour*'s summer 2000 headline, "Could Your Period Give You Cancer?" After pulling the reader in with this dramatic question, the article cites a recent research finding that some oral contraceptives have been shown to diminish risk of ovarian cancer. It is, of course, a substantial inferential leap from that finding to suggest that menstruation causes cancer.

A more typical article promoting menstrual suppression appeared in *Ladies Home Journal* in the spring of 2001. Writer Sharlene K. Johnson characterizes the elimination of monthly periods as "a dream come true." The article goes on to cite Coutinho's book and several medical doctors who use birth control pills to suppress their own menstrual cycles and encourage the practice in their patients. It is argued that convenience and the prevention of ovarian cancer are the best reasons to do so. A similar article appeared at the same time in *Redbook,* quoting Coutinho's sometime US collaborator, Sheldon Segal, claiming that half of all women's complaints to gynecologists deal with menstruation. Jill Huppert, an M.D. who suppresses her own cycles with oral contraceptives, is quoted saying, "I can't imagine having a period every four weeks. That's the stupidest thing I've ever heard of, and I won't do it" (James-Enger, 2001). It is hard for a reader to be surprised that so many women seem eager for chemical suppression of their periods when such condemnation of menstruation is expressed by their physicians.

In 2002, *Elle* published a short blurb about the forthcoming birth control pill, Seasonale, then pending FDA approval (McCarthy, 2002). This article touted the advantage of saving money on menstrual supplies—neglecting to point out that the cost of the additional pills will likely equal any savings in tampons and menstrual pads. Given that many insurance companies won't cover the use of contraceptive pills for contraception, it seems unlikely that the pills will be covered when prescribed for menstrual suppression for convenience reasons, making them an added expense for users without contraceptive need who simply want to stop menstruating. (Additionally, women are likely to experience spotting and irregular bleeding for the first year of use and thus may still use menstrual products.)

Articles similar to these pieces from *Glamour, Ladies Home Journal, Redbook,* and *Elle* have also appeared in *Shape, Cosmopolitan, The Boston Globe, The Washington Post, The Los Angeles Times, The Guardian, The New Yorker,* and *The Globe and Mail.* Few mainstream media outlets have published rebuttals to Coutinho and Segal's case for menstrual suppression. A systematic study of 22 articles about menstrual suppression from the popular press revealed considerably more attention and more positive attention to the case for menstrual suppression than to the case against it. Advocates were quoted twice as often as opponents (Johnston-Robledo, Barnack, and Wares, in press).

There are, however, numerous sound arguments against using hormones for long-term menstrual suppression. A few have even appeared in mainstream news media. Jean Elson, University of New Hampshire sociologist, pointed out in *Newsday* that most of the reasons advocates promote hormonal menstrual suppression—hygiene issues, embarrassment, expense, interference with athletic performance, and convenience while traveling—are social, not medical, problems (Elson, 2002).

In the *Canadian Women's Health Newsletter,* Kathleen O'Grady critically summarized Coutinho's syllogistic logic as follows: "since menstruation exists for the purpose of prolific childbearing, and repeated childbirth is no longer necessary, then menstruation is now 'obsolete'" (O'Grady, 2002). Therefore, menstruation should be suppressed in all reproductive-aged women. Jerilynn Prior, Professor of Endocrinology at University of British Columbia, explains that the logic of taking ovulation-suppressing hormones to eliminate menstruation reflects an incomplete understanding of the relationship between menstruation and ovulation. Studies of runners and women with physically demanding lives, such as present-day hunter-gatherer tribes of the Kalahari, show that ovulation and menstruation do not always or necessarily coincide. That is, regular periods can and do occur with no ovulation or with disturbed ovulation (Prior, 2000). Hormonal contraceptives, whether pills, injections, skin patches, or vaginal devices, work by suppressing ovulation. This may or may not also suppress menstruation; in fact, about half of women in clinical trials for these drugs report what is known as "breakthrough bleeding" (Kelley, 2003). This erratic and unpredictable bleeding is the primary reason women have dropped out of clinical trials for Seasonale and other oral contraceptives (Kalb, 2003; Kelley, 2003). The side effect of menstrual irregularity is the most commonly cited reason women give for stopping use of hormonal contraceptives altogether (Potter, 2001).

Many proponents of menstrual suppression assert that there is simply no reason for modern women to menstruate, other than for brief periods when trying to conceive. However, others have argued that enabling childbearing is not the only purpose of menstruation. At least three additional biological reasons have been posited to explain why menstruation persists.

In a controversial *Quarterly Review of Biology* article in 1993, Margie Profet argued that from an evolutionary standpoint, menstruation would simply not have endured if it did not serve some useful biological function. Her studies noted that menstrual blood differs from other human blood, primarily in that it contains macrophages, immune cells that fight pathogens in the uterine cavity. Profet asserted that menstruation functions to protect the uterus and keep female reproductive organs free of contaminants, most notably from those contained in or carried by sperm (Profet, 1993).

Disputing Profet's assertions, Beverly Strassmann argued that humans and other primates menstruate because cyclically shedding the unused endometrium is energetically less costly than maintaining it in a constant state of readiness for implantation (Strassmann, 1996). Some endocrinologists believe that an additional reason for menstruation is to give the body a break from estrogen (Prior, 2000). The three or four days at the beginning of the menstrual cycle when estrogen is lowest (during flow) prevent breast tenderness. The only situation in nature in which estrogen levels are continuously high is during pregnancy; however, the levels of progesterone at this time are even higher and thus counterbalance the effects of continuous estrogen (Prior, 2003, personal communication). Prior (2000) has also noted that menstrual cycle problems such as premenstrual symptoms, migraines, breast pain, and severe cramps are caused by low levels of progesterone in proportion to levels of estrogen. Oral contraceptives are often prescribed to treat these problems and eliminate menstruation by increasing the amount of estrogen in a woman's body.

As O'Grady (2002) notes, independent assessment of Coutinho's work, preferably by people or organizations who won't benefit directly from increased sales of hormonal contraceptives, is needed. As Profet, Prior, and other researchers have indicated, menstruation serves important biological functions in addition to its role in fertility and reproduction. Menstruation affects the entire endocrine system, as well as cardiovascular health and bone strength. The relationship of menstruation and ovulation to women's overall health and well-being should not be dismissed or minimized without further research.

One might have hoped that the 2003 introduction of Seasonale would have sparked such study, as well as additional criticism and debate among experts. The American College of Obstetricians and Gynecologists (ACOG) has not offered a public position on Seasonale, although a Gallup poll of 301 women obstetrician-gynecologists conducted for ACOG found that nearly 99 percent of them consider using oral contraceptives for menstrual suppression to be safe. More than half of those surveyed said they had tried it themselves (Schneider, 2004). There was, however, much discussion among scholars in the social sciences—for example, the 2003 meeting of the Society for Menstrual Cycle Research devoted several sessions to this topic—but the mass media coverage has been nearly one-sided, as noted above (Johnston-Robledo, Barnack, and Wares, in press).

Although some news reports note that the drug is not universally endorsed, potential risks and side effects are frequently minimized.

They are also attributed to lone crusaders, such as psychiatrist Susan Rako, author of *No More Periods? The Risks of Menstrual Suppression and Other Cutting-Edge Issues About Hormones and Women's Health*. Rako is concerned about increased risk of osteoporosis, heart attacks, strokes, cancer, and heart problems in women who use extended-cycle oral contraceptives (Kelley, 2003; McCullough, 2003; "Pill Puts Periods on Hold," 2003; Rako, 2003). Johnston-Robledo and her colleagues (2003) noted a subtle pattern in the quoting of experts in media coverage of Seasonale: Obstetrician-gynecologists quoted in news articles are nearly unanimous in endorsing menstrual suppression, while experts who question its safety or oppose it are usually psychiatrists or psychologists. Given the consistency of this pattern, I suspect that this differential argument from authority was strategically developed by public relations experts in the employ of the drug's manufacturer.[1]

Rako elaborates safety concerns of constant estrogen and suppressed menstruation in her book. She argues that in addition to the risks cited above, "hormonal interruption of the menstrual cycle affects female-male partner choice, is intimately linked with factors that determine immune mechanisms, and can ultimately even detrimentally affect the human species" (Rako, 2003: 20). In support of this thesis, she cites research on pheromones and the major histocompatibility complex that reported radical alterations in women's odor assessment and preferences when the subjects were taking oral contraceptives. Rako predicts profound effects on human relationships if menstrual suppression with hormonal methods becomes widespread.

Rako is also concerned about the interaction of estrogen with other hormones; for example, she argues that increased estrogen will result in decreases in dehydroepiandrosterone (DHEA) and available testosterone. Testosterone, asserts Rako (2003), is essential for women's health and quality of life, as it affects energy, mood, and sexual sensitivity and response.

Rako also points out two little-known health advantages of regular menstruation: reduced blood pressure (during half of the cycle) and reduction of iron stores, which reduces risks for heart attack and strokes. Although Rako cites less detail in support of her concern with bone remodeling (Rako, 2003), ovulatory menstrual cycles are known to be linked to the bones' ability to accrete minerals and thicken (Prior, 2004b). Winnifred Cutler, president and founder of the Athena Institute for Women's Wellness, has also published concerns about how suppression of ovulation may lead to early osteoporosis;

the regulation of bone remodeling is closely linked to hormone cycles and other factors (Cutler, 2002).

Rako's most important critique effectively summarizes all of these issues: She notes that the "no more bleeding" message of the anti-period movement really means no more menstrual cycle, and that the two are not synonymous. Rako writes, "The intricate interplay of hormones that rise and fall in a monthly pattern have remarkable effects on every organ system in the body and are at the foundation of natural and sexual selection in the human species" (2003: 31).

Although I can't get as worked up about the potential pheromone issue as Rako, I find little to dispute in the substance of most of her other criticisms. There seems to be little understanding or appreciation of the complexity of the menstrual system in the media coverage of menstrual suppression and even less research on the long-term effects. I do, however, find it strange and a little disappointing that Rako is the most prominently featured critic of menstrual suppression in the mainstream media.

My disappointment stems from the quality of *No More Periods*; it is not a particularly well-written book. The strength of Rako's argument is diminished by weak organization, irrelevant personal tangents (such as the memory of a medical professor who bought seamed stockings for his wife long after they'd gone out of fashion), a patronizing tone (evidenced in such warnings as "There will be no quiz at the end of the section" [p. 64] and "Stick with it. While the explanation has some complexity, I believe that you can get your mind around this one without a full case of 'the boggles'" [p. 67]), serious overuse of boldface type, and perhaps most damaging in my estimation, an overreliance on the "don't mess with nature" argument.

The fact that something exists in nature speaks to neither its advantages nor its disadvantages; this seems especially obvious with respect to health and medical issues. As a feminist cultural critic and as a beneficiary of numerous innovations of Western medicine that have changed what some might regard as my "natural" state, I take particular issue with Rako's frequent references to female nature and feminine intuition.

More important for my larger point, I'm frustrated by the appearance of Rako as a lone crusader. The Canadian Women's Health Network (CWHN) has taken a public stance against menstrual suppression that has received little media attention (at least in the United States). A few others with concerns about menstrual suppression have received limited media coverage. In an interview with National

Public Radio's "All Things Considered," Arthur Caplan, bioethicist at University of Pennsylvania, questioned the introduction of a drug to intervene in something that "isn't clearly dysfunctional" (Seigel and Jones, 2003). Well-known physician Susan Love, of the Susan Love Breast Cancer Research Foundation, has questioned the drug's safety on a long-term basis. She told *Newsweek,* "One of the things the HRT [hormone replacement therapy] debacle showed us is that we just can't assume safety" (quoted in Kalb, 2003). Love is critical of using oral contraceptives for menstrual suppression, asserting on her website that the pills may increase the risk of breast cancer (Love, 2003). Christine Hitchcock and Jerilynn Prior have pointed out that the even though the studies that Barr Laboratories submitted to the FDA assessed long-term use of Seasonale, there is a selection bias that may contaminate the data. The majority of subjects in these studies were women who were current users of traditional birth control pills and thus already tolerant of the chemicals in oral contraceptives. Hitchcock and Prior caution against extrapolating from the success of the trials in this group of women to those who do not use oral contraceptives (Hitchcock and Prior, 2003).

The "HRT debacle" referenced by Susan Love is the closure of a component of the Women's Health Initiative (WHI) study of the risks and benefits of estrogen and progestin supplements for post-menopausal women (conducted under the umbrella of the National Institutes of Health [NIH]) in the summer of 2002. The clinical trials were stopped because findings indicated increased risk of invasive breast cancer as well as increases in coronary heart disease, stroke, and pulmonary embolism. Although the hormone supplements provided some benefit in fewer hip fractures and reduced risk of colon cancer, the benefits were not sufficient to outweigh the risks (NIH, 2002). In early 2004, a second arm of the WHI study was closed a year earlier than expected. Although the data showed that estrogen alone does not appear to affect (either increase or decrease) heart disease, estrogen alone does appear to increase the risk of stroke (NIH, 2004).

Critics may wish to dismiss comparisons between HRT and oral contraceptives, pointing to the forty years of pill usage by US women with few ill effects, but the long-term effects of additional nine weeks of synthetic estrogens each year remain unknown. The clinical tests that won Barr FDA approval included fewer than 300 women, monitored for only one year (Anderson and Hait, 2003). As noted above, the majority of subjects in these studies were women who were current users of traditional birth control pills, and thus the success of the trials in this group of women may not extend to all women (Hitchcock and Prior, 2003). This hardly represents a ringing endorsement for long-term safety.

Also, even though the birth control pill has been used with relative safety by millions of US women, there is no precedent for continuous use of such large doses of hormones from the teen years to menopause. Women currently use oral contraceptives from their teens until their late twenties or early thirties, when they typically complete their families, and then they choose a more permanent method of contraception (tubal ligation for themselves or vasectomy for their male partner). Seasonale is presented to consumers as a lifestyle drug that women will want to use from menarche to menopause.

The market for lifestyle drugs—"a pharmaceutical which is taken not to relieve or cure a medical condition, but to improve the quality of life of the person taking it" (Quinion, 1998)—is rapidly expanding. The market is currently estimated at $23 billion. Market research firms such as Mind Branch expect the market for lifestyle drugs to continue to grow at least through 2008 (Mind Branch, 2003).

Lifestyle drugs are a subject of debate, both in terms of whether they should be covered by private and government health insurance (Stolberg, 2005) and what influence they have in reframing "complaints of the healthy into conditions of the sick" (Moynihan, quoted in "Do We Need Lifestyle Drugs?", 2003). Nancy Fugate Woods (2005) recently posited that the phrase "quality of life" has been successfully co-opted by drug marketers to mask increasing medicalization of women, especially in the advertising of hormone therapy for postmenopausal women. The original Barr Laboratories website for Seasonale—no longer online—emphasized that taking Seasonale for menstrual suppression was a "lifestyle choice."

Selling Seasonale

There has been some limited public criticism of the discourse rather than the drug: A 2003 statement by the National Women's Health Network (NWHN) on the use of extended-cycle contraceptives for menstrual suppression objects not to the availability of the drug, but to "the way that it is being discussed in the medical community and may be presented to women by health care providers" (NWHN, 2003). The NWHN is concerned that benefits of the drug may be overstated or medical need exaggerated, resulting in increased negative attitudes toward menstruation, especially among young women.

The organization urges Barr Laboratories and clinicians not to "get ahead of the research and science," pointing out that the demonstrated correlation in epidemiological research between frequency of menstruation or ovulation and some reproductive cancers does not indicate causality (NWHN, 2003).

The Canadian Women's Health Network (CWHN) has made even stronger statements in opposition to menstrual suppression. The Winter/ Spring 2004 edition of the CWHN Newsletter featured an essay by epidemiologist Abby Lippman that discussed menstrual suppression and HRT for menopause as examples of "neo-medicalization"—a renewed medicalizing of physiological events of women's lives (menstruation and menopause) by labeling them as illnesses and prescribing medical treatment (Lippman, 2004). In the summer of 2004, the CWHN published and distributed a poster with a visual and textual critique of Seasonale and menstrual suppression. The poster features the powerful headline "We're not sick—we're women" superimposed against an image of a tampon, and includes several quotes from news articles noting that no long-term studies have assessed the safety of menstrual suppression (see Figure 5.1).

NWHN is among few critics of the frequently asserted claim that the elimination of menstrual cycles is more natural than frequent menstruation because prehistoric women did not menstruate with the frequency of modern women. It is cited repeatedly (see, for example, Coutinho, 1999; Kalb, 2003; Westphal, 2002) that prehistoric women had fewer than 100 periods over the course of a lifetime, rather than the average of 450 for women today. Mitchell Creinin, director of family planning in the obstetrics and gynecology department at University of Pittsburgh told a *Pittsburgh Post-Gazette* reporter that "[w]hat's natural is for women to have one to two periods a year and to either be breast-feeding or pregnant the rest of the time. Monthly periods are an artifact of modern contraception" (quoted in Hoffman, 2003). The NWHN statement notes that "[w]hile it is accurate to say that women menstruate more today than they have at other times, the implication that monthly menstruation is unnatural is unfounded" (NWHN, 2003).

It is also true that infrequency of menstruation is only a partial picture of a prehistoric woman's natural life. Sylvia Westphal (2002) notes that our prehistoric ancestors were hungry more often than most humans today, but few today would assert that hunger should therefore be our preferred normal state. It is also well known that our ancestors had an average life span less than half of what young

Figure 5.1   Canadian Women's Health Network Poster, 2004

Source: Used with permission of Canadian Women's Health Network.

women today can expect, yet no one today is urging death at age 40 as more "natural" than old age.

Or, as Geneva Kachman exclaimed, "I really don't care if hunter-gatherer women had only two periods per year, for a grand total of 28 periods in a lifetime. I am a writer-thinker woman living in capitalist, globalizing, United States of America, year 2003" (Kachman, 2003b). Kachman appreciates her period for the opportunity it provides to withdraw from that world momentarily. Other women—especially writers and artists—have noted feeling extra creativity during or just before their menstrual flow (Culpepper, 1991; Francia, 1991; Ouellette, 1991; Owen, 1991). Emily Martin's (1987) anthropological study of modern women's menstrual experience theorizes about how menstruation affects women's sense of time, noting that the modern workplace is not configured to accommodate menstruation. (See also Chapter 4.)

Menstruation has such strong negative connotations in US culture that few women can cite positive changes associated with menstruation (Koff, Rierdan, and Stubbs, 1990; Nichols, 1995). Press coverage of Seasonale exploits these perceptions; in 2003, many articles in the mainstream press opened with a paragraph about the inconvenience of menstruation, not with an argument about health or illness concerns, as these examples illustrate:

- "Menstrual periods are unpleasant, inconvenient, and expensive" (McCullough, 2003).
- "Hate having a menstrual period or the yucky side effects that may come with it? A new drug arriving in stores in late October will allow women to avoid all but four periods a year" ("Pill Puts Periods on Hold," 2003).
- "The best thing about a menstrual period is . . . nothing. It is painful, bloats tummies, brings out the inner witch, and is inconvenient" (Lewis, 2003).
- "Imagine a world where being a woman means never having to say you're sorry because PMS ruined another romantic weekend; where your period doesn't dictate your wardrobe for one-quarter of your childbearing years; where you can wear white without fear 365 days a year" (Philbin, 2003)

Such remarks occur over and over in media coverage of Seasonale. It is presented as so well understood as to be unquestionable that no woman would choose to menstruate, that there is nothing at all positive or beneficial about having a period. Carole Ben-Maimon, the president and chief operating officer of Seasonale's manufacturer, is quoted in a company press release presenting the drug's primary purpose as convenience: "With today's approval of Seasonale, women have a new choice when deciding on oral contraception. *For those women who prefer the convenience of fewer periods,* Seasonale offers a safe and effective alternative to the 28-day oral contraceptive regimen" (Cox, 2003: 1, emphasis added). These pronouncements echo the sentiments of ads for feminine hygiene products (discussed in Chapter 2) and reinforce their messages of concealment.

Barr Laboratories should be credited with skillful manipulation not only of menstruation but of media as well. Public relations specialists distinguish between "earned media," that is, public relations coverage, and "paid media," or advertising (Earle, 2000). Dozens of articles about the drug were in print and online months before the 250-person pharmaceutical sales team was unleashed November 18, 2003 ("Barr Begins Detailing Seasonale to Physicians," 2003). By late December 2003, a Google search on the word *Seasonale* quickly returned more than 10,000 hits. Direct-to-consumer advertisements appeared nationwide by the spring of 2004, with the slogan, "Fewer periods. More possibilities." Seasonale continued to receive earned media coverage in newspapers and magazines in 2005.

Even articles that appear to present the opposition or to question the safety of Seasonale ultimately endorse it, as in the Salon.com article by Jennifer Fried (reprinted in *The Guardian* for a larger audience). The article is subtitled, "But Is It Safe To Staunch the Flow?" Although Fried dutifully quotes Susan Rako calling menstrual suppression "the largest uncontrolled experiment in medical history," her final answer to the question in her subtitle appears to be, "Who cares? We can!" Most disturbing is her attribution of feminist motives to Seasonale's backers: Fried asserts that "*the* feminist case for menstrual suppression" is that women will no longer miss work or school due to menstrual pain (2003: 3, emphasis added). Although feminists vary in their attitudes toward menstruation and menstrual suppression, few have argued that missing work or school occasionally is a major source of women's oppression comparable to unequal pay or gendered violence.

Attitude Adjustments

The negativity toward menstruation expressed in media coverage and promotion of Seasonale is neither new nor surprising. Social scientists have documented a long history of negative attitudes toward menstruation (Chrisler et al., 1994; Koff, Rierdan, and Stubbs, 1990; Lander, 1988; Laws, 1990). In fact, research efforts to identify positive aspects of the menstrual cycle are complicated by the pervasiveness of this cultural pessimism (Nichols, 1995).

Researchers have undertaken the challenge nevertheless. Chrisler and her colleagues (1994) have been particularly innovative: Inspired by Delaney, Lupton, and Toth's (1988) offhand speculation about how results might change if a Menstrual Joy Questionnaire were administered instead of the widely used Menstrual Distress Questionnaire (MDQ) to assess women's experiences of menstruation, they developed just such an instrument. Developed in 1968, the MDQ was the first standardized method for collecting data about menstrual cycle symptomatology (Moos, 1968). Moos's MDQ assesses a respondent's experience of forty-seven specific symptoms from eight distinct clusters of symptoms: pain, concentration, behavioral change, autonomic reactions, water retention, negative affect, arousal, and control. Women are asked to rate their experience of each of the forty-seven symptoms on a six-point scale ranging from no experience of the symptom to acute or partially disabling experience of the symptom, and to complete these ratings separately for premenstrual, menstrual, and intermenstrual phases of her cycle.

Chrisler et al. (1994) used Delaney et al.'s ten positive effects of menstruation to develop a Menstrual Joy Questionnaire, aptly nicknamed MJQ. The MJQ uses the same format to measure high spirits, increased sexual desire, vibrant activity, revolutionary zeal, intense concentration, feelings of affection, self-confidence, sense of euphoria, creativity, and feelings of power. Their first test of the measure found that women who completed the MJQ a week in advance of completing the MDQ reported more positive menstrual changes on the MDQ and higher scores on a third instrument, the Menstrual Attitude Questionnaire (MAQ), than women who completed the MDQ before the MJQ. Participants also reported "that they were surprised or incredulous; most had not previously considered positive aspects of the menstrual cycle" (Chrisler et al., 1994: 375). Although subsequent testing of the MJQ showed poor reliability, the testers assert "the shortcomings as a measure should not detract from the strong effects the scale seems to have as a stimulus" (Heard et al., 1999: 136).

Both the MDQ and the MJQ are intended to assess symptomatology. The third instrument, the MAQ, was developed to measure women's and men's attitudes toward menstruation (Brooks-Gunn and Ruble, 1980). In their efforts to develop an instrument that conceptualized attitudes toward menstruation as multidimensional and as both positive and negative, the researchers identified five distinct attitude dimensions: menstruation as debilitating, menstruation as bothersome, menstruation as natural, menstruation as predictable, and denial of any effects of menstruation. They acknowledged that additional attitude dimensions may also exist. Among their findings in testing the instrument, Brooks-Gunn and Ruble (1980) discovered that perceiving menstruation as natural does not negate a perception of menstruation as bothersome. They also found that while some women perceive menstruation as debilitating, two-thirds of the women they surveyed did not. Also, very few women denied any effects of menstruation.

A recent survey by the Association of Reproductive Health Professionals (ARHP), which was funded by Barr Laboratories, sought to assess women's attitudes toward menstrual suppression. Interestingly, the researchers used neither the MAQ nor the MDQ, developing their own questionnaire instead to assess both attitudes and symptomatology. Although their survey did include some items allowing for expression of positive attitudes toward menstruation (e.g., "In some ways I enjoy my period"), the ARHP findings report that 71 percent of women do not enjoy getting their period each month, and 62 percent would be interested in stopping their period "if it were safe and free" (ARHP, 2003). However, only a small minority reported severe painful symptoms with their period. Although the results are not correlated in this manner, the ARHP findings appear consistent with Hoyt and Andrist's (2003) findings that women's attitudes toward their menstrual cycles are a better predictor of their interest in menstrual suppression than their symptomatology. In other words, the more negative a woman's attitude toward her period, the more interested in menstrual suppression she is likely to be. Unsurprisingly, both women and health professionals surveyed in the ARHP study overwhelmingly favor additional study of the long-term safety of menstrual suppression.

One is left to wonder about the relationship between these negative attitudes and women's knowledge of menstruation. Koff, Rierdan, and Stubbs' (1990) surveys of women college students found startling inadequacies and errors in their knowledge of menstruation. Although most of the women had some idea of the cause of menstruation, many expressed confusion about the specific glands and organs involved, the role of hormones, and the process of ovulation. In fact, the respondents seemed unable to distinguish between the ovulation, premenstrual, and menstrual phases of the cycle.

That these findings occur during a time of increasing societal openness about menstruation and greater frankness in the menstrual education of girls is telling. Although only 5 to 10 percent of adolescent girls at the end of the twentieth century experienced their first period with no advance knowledge of menstruation, their menstrual education still cannot be considered comprehensive or complete (Kissling, 1996a). Menstrual education has been criticized for inadequate attention to emotional aspects of menstruation (Brumberg, 1997; Kissling, 1996a), but the Koff, Rierdan, and Stubbs (1990) findings point to surprising deficiencies in knowledge about physiology, fertility, and reproduction among today's young women.

More than 30 percent of the college women in Koff, Rierdan, and Stubbs' (1990) sample could not provide even a rudimentary definition of menstruation or an accurate characterization of ovulation. Although a small number of subjects attributed some positive emotional changes to ovulation, most described dysphoric changes. While these subjects were more likely to assign positive changes to ovulation than to menstruation, their responses contradict well-established research findings indicating heightened feelings of well-being and amiability during ovulation. The authors attribute these responses to the pervasiveness of negative stereotypes of menstruation.

Cultural negativity about menstruation is surely one of the factors that helps explain women's ignorance of menstruation. The focus in both the scholarship of menstruation and in the popular press about the four or five days of premenstrual changes is another factor. Doreen Asso (1983) has asserted that two-thirds of the menstrual cycle is virtually unstudied in comparison. In fact, "[t]here is no general recognition that every month the cycle turns through a myriad of changes which for most of the time create in women an entirely positive physical and psychological climate" (Asso, 1983: xiv).

An Ounce of Prevention or a Month of Pills?

Even menstrual suppression's strongest critics note that it can be beneficial for women who suffer from severe menstrual pain or conditions such as endometriosis or severe premenstrual syndrome. However, before taking potentially dangerous hormones, women and their physicians would be wise to consider the possibility of alternative causes and treatments for these problems. As noted in Chapter 4, clinical studies reveal the most successful treatments for PMS to be exercise and/or calcium supplements. Current theories about endometriosis suggest it may be triggered by excessive estrogen, at least in part via animal products consumed in the typical US diet (Mills and Vernon, 1999). Some women have found relief from painful symptoms of endometriosis by changing their diet and their lifestyle.

Clearly, many of the menstruation-related health problems menstrual suppression purports to solve are not caused by menstruation, but by US society's prescribed treatment of menstruation. As historians of women's health have documented, the promotion of Seasonale isn't the first time the pharmaceutical and health-care industries have recommended hormonal adjustments for problems best remedied by attitude adjustments.

Women's health activist and historian Barbara Seaman (2003) has labeled the sixty-five-year history of marketing, prescribing, and selling synthetic estrogens to women *The Greatest Experiment Ever Performed on Women* in her recent book with this title. The formula for cheap, powerful, oral estrogen first became publicly available in 1938, and estrogens have since been prescribed to women for the nondisease of aging, the "hot flashes" associated with menopause, contraception, and miscarriage prevention. Seaman calls the prescription and marketing of estrogens to women the "greatest experiment" because, "for all these years, they have been used, in the main, for what doctors and scientists hope or believe they can do, not for what they *know* the products can do" (2003: 5, emphasis in original).

The risks of estrogen supplementation have been known and documented since the introduction of synthetic estrogen: The same British biochemist who published the formula in 1938 also warned of increased risk of breast and endometrial cancer. In 1947, Dr. Saul Gusberg asserted that estrogen is to endometrial cancer what we now know cigarettes are to lung cancer (Seaman, 2003). Yet physicians continue to prescribe estrogens, and many women continue to swallow them without asking questions, and the estrogen experiment continues:

> Here is the essence of the estrogen experiment. For forty years drug companies, scientists, and researchers have been playing carrot-and-stick with women's lives. They hold out poorly substantiated claims for estrogen's health benefits, which buys them time as they try to develop the proof to back up the claims. But the fact remains that after all these years, and with countless deaths attributable to estrogen via cancers, cardiovascular complications, blood clots, and other health problems, including asthma and gall-bladder disease, the evidence isn't there. If the data is there, women must demand to see it before agreeing to put more pills into our bodies. (Seaman, 2003: 204)

It is surprising that the closure of the WHI studies has not provoked suspicion of other uses of estrogens. Although formulations of oral contraceptives vary from one another and from HRT drugs, the WHI findings should give pause to women considering relying on birth control pills for menstrual suppression. The drugs are not directly comparable, as most HRT drugs contain animal-derived estrogen (Premarin® gets its name from its source, *preg*nant *mar*e ur*ine* [Seaman, 2003]) while birth control pills contain synthetic estrogen, and most formulations also contain some variation of progesterone. But oral contraceptives are typically four to seven times stronger than hormone replacement drugs (Society of Obstetricians and Gynaecologists of Canada, n.d.). Although oral contraceptives are known to reduce risk of ovarian cancer, the relationship between them and breast cancer is not clear (Boston Women's Health Collective, 1998; National Cancer Institute, 2003). It is quite likely that the only reason increased breast cancer risk has not been seen in women who use oral contraceptives is that young women, the primary users, rarely get breast cancer and no population of birth control pill users have both used the drug long-term *and* been followed for study at the ages when breast cancer is more common (Prior, 2004a).

New information is continually developing regarding the relationships between hormones and cancers. On July 29, 2005, the International Agency for Research on Cancer (IARC), a division of the World Health Organization, announced that based on their review of the published evidence, the IARC Monographs Working Group has concluded that combined estrogen-progestin contraceptives and combined estrogen-progestin menopausal therapy are carcinogenic to humans. The IARC uses five classifications of carcinogenicity: (1) carcinogenic to humans, (2) probably carcinogenic to humans, (3) possibly carcinogenic to humans, (4) not classifiable as to its carcinogenicity to humans, and (5) probably not carcinogenic to humans. Combined estrogen-progestin drugs received the first classification. While the IARC press release does note that users of combined oral contraceptives face lowered risks of endometrial and ovarian cancer, they face higher risks of liver cancer and cervical cancer. The risk of cervical cancer increases with duration of use (Gaudin, 2005). As of this writing in 2005, hormonal menstrual suppression is on its way to becoming the next uncontrolled estrogen experiment.

Before closing this chapter, a point of clarification is in order: My primary objections to extended-use contraceptives are my belief that the risks of long-term menstrual suppression are not known and my belief that menstruation is not a disease in need of a remedy. I am *not* opposed to the use of hormonal contraception as such; it is a valid and appropriate choice for many women. Like Margaret Sanger (1920), I believe "[n]o woman can call herself free who does not own and control her body. No woman can call herself free until she can choose consciously whether she will or will not be a mother." I want that freedom to include fully informed choices based on the most reliable information available.

Note

1. Of course, such speculation is difficult to prove.

6

Tampon Safety Debates and Product Alternatives

WHEN DISPOSABLE TAMPONS WERE FIRST INTRODUCED TO THE consumer market in the 1930s, the only question of risk in using tampons was whether the tapered, narrow cotton plugs would pierce a hymen or promote masturbation, and those weren't health risks but social concerns. Nearly fifty years later, in 1980, tampons were at the center of a public health scandal in the United States when thirty-eight women died from toxic shock syndrome (TSS), believed to have been contracted through use of super-absorbent tampons (Houppert, 1999). TSS is a rare but potentially fatal blood infection caused by a bacterial toxin. Its symptoms often come on suddenly and include high fever, vomiting, diarrhea, a sunburn-like rash, red eyes, dizziness, lightheadedness, muscle aches, and drops in blood pressure, which may cause fainting or shock.

It is unknown why some women exposed to *Staphylococcus aureus* will develop TSS and others will not; high-absorbency tampons, especially when worn for many hours, are believed to increase a woman's risk of developing TSS (Boston Women's Health Collective, 1998; Tierno, 2001). Researchers at Harvard Medical School believe two kinds of fiber used in tampons in the late 1970s and early 1980s fostered the development of the bacterial toxin that causes TSS. The fibers, polyester foam and polyacrylate rayon, do this by leeching magnesium from the vagina, which creates a suitable environment for the toxin to grow and thrive ("Doctors Say They've Found Cause of Toxic Shock," 1985). Researchers at New York University Medical Center found that menstruation and tampons made with polyacrylates created the ideal climate for biological, chemical, and physical factors to combine and transform those fibers into "hundreds of 'toxin factories' in every super absorbent tampon" (Tierno, 2001:

80). Procter & Gamble's Rely brand tampons, which included these new super-absorbent synthetic fibers, were linked to TSS and withdrawn from the market in 1980 (Houppert, 1999). In 1985, Playtex and Tambrands voluntarily withdrew products using polyacrylate rayon from the market (Havemann, 1987). All US tampon manufacturers stopped using polyester foam and polyacrylate rayon during the 1980s (Condor, 2000).

It took seven years from the first TSS death linked to tampons and substantial pressure from consumer and feminist activists until the FDA began requiring tampon manufacturers to use consistent ratings of absorbency and advising women to use the lowest-rated tampon necessary to manage their flow (Havemann, 1987; Houppert, 1999). Tampon manufacturers also began to publish warnings on tampon packaging and inserts, advising wearers to change tampons frequently and not to wear them overnight. Although manufacturers denied any association between tampons and TSS, they began to produce lower absorbency products, pulling high absorbency tampons from the market by the end of the 1980s (Rome and Wolhandler, 1991). The warnings appear on the packaging and inserts of all tampon brands today, now required by the FDA (Knopper, 2003).

Throughout the early 1980s, most documented cases of TSS were found in young, white women who were menstruating at the time of onset. Almost 80 percent of cases identified in 1982 were menstruation-associated, and of these, 99 percent of the women were tampon users (Centers for Disease Control [CDC], 1983). By the end of the 1990s, CDC surveillance data showed a marked decline in total cases of TSS and an increase in nonmenstrual TSS (Haijeh et al., 1999). In 1990, the CDC stated that "[t]he precise mechanism by which Rely tampons increased the risk of TSS is unknown. The increased risk associated with high absorbency tampons is also poorly understood; high absorbency may be a surrogate for another effect" (CDC, 1990). The 1999 CDC study suggested several possible reasons for the decline in TSS in general and menstruation-related TSS in particular: reduced tampon absorbency, standardized tampon labeling, greater awareness of TSS, and the "proliferation of educational materials for women, including tampon package inserts" (Haijeh et al., 1999: 809). Philip M. Tierno, Jr., one of the microbiologists who first made the connection between TSS and tampons, believes the decline is due in no small part to underreporting and to the strict definition required by the CDC for reporting (Tierno, 2001).

In the late 1990s, tampons became a public health issue again, as a rumor circulated on the Internet that manufacturers included asbestos among the ingredients. Allegedly, asbestos would increase vaginal bleeding among tampon users and thus increase tampon sales. FDA materials have declared since at least 1999 that "[a]sbestos is not an ingredient in any US brand of tampon, nor is it associated with the fibers used in making tampons" (FDA, 1999). The assertion has also been debunked on Snopes.com, Urbanlegends.com, and Quackwatch—three esteemed and frequently used websites for debunking Internet hoaxes and rumors. Variations of the e-mail message continue to circulate, however, and appeared in the e-mail in-box of a Nova Scotia doctor's wife in the spring of 2003. Her husband wrote a column repeating the falsity of the asbestos allegations in Toronto's *Medical Post* (MacLean, 2003).

The rumor of asbestos-infested tampons persists on the Internet, much like the urban legends of "The Hook" and "The Kentucky Fried Rat" persist in oral tradition. Folklore scholars consider urban legends to be illustrative of a community's fears and anxieties, or tensions the society is struggling with. The asbestos rumor is similar to other urban legends of contamination, such as the pervasive tales of insects or rodents in packaged food or foreign matter in restaurant food, suggestive of fears of corporate disregard for consumer safety (Brunvand, 1981). This rumor emphasizes corporate greed at the expense of women's health and safety and thus reflects suspicion of femcare manufacturers.

Despite the persistence of this rumor and their own criticism of the femcare industry, the asbestos legend was never taken seriously by anti-tampon activists (Chris Bobel, February 2004, personal communication). Women's health activists found allegations of the presence of dioxin—a dangerous chemical created as a by-product of elemental chlorine bleaching—in tampons are much more serious and compelling. These allegations first surfaced in 1989, when the British organization Women's Environmental Network (WEN) published *The Sanitary Protection Scandal*. A similar book appeared in North America in 1992, when Liz Armstrong and Adrienne Scott published *Whitewash: Exposing the Health and Environmental Dangers of Women's Sanitary Products and Disposable Diapers*. These books asserted that dioxin is present in paper products, in wood pulp, in the process wastewater from wood pulp manufacturing, and in the sludge left over after processing.

What Is Dioxin?

Dioxin is best known in the United States for its role in Vietnam as a component of Agent Orange, the herbicide used by the US Air

Force to defoliate river embankments and to limit vegetation around US base camps during the Vietnam War (Wildavsky and Swedlow, 1995). Dioxin has since become one of the world's most studied environmental chemicals (Silbergeld, 1992). Dioxin is actually not a single chemical, but a family of chemicals with similar properties and toxicity. There are seventy-five different dioxins, the most toxic of which is 2, 3, 7, 8-tetrachlorodibenzo-*p*-dioxin, or TCDD.

Dioxins are not manufactured or used, but form unintentionally as a chemical by-product of polyvinyl chloride production or of any process using chlorine. Dioxin is also produced by combustion of organic materials. Dioxin is known to be a human carcinogen, as well as toxic to human and animal reproductive, developmental, immune, and endocrine systems. It is highly persistent, and it accumulates in the tissues of animals, with the highest concentrations in fatty tissues. Although dioxin levels in the environment have declined following Environmental Protection Agency (EPA) regulatory controls implemented in the past twenty years, dioxin is so effectively dispersed throughout the planet that all living things contain measurable amounts. The half-life of dioxins in human beings is estimated to range from seven to eleven years (Birnbaum and Cummings, 2002; EPA, 2001; Gibbs, 1995; Silbergeld, 1992).

According to EPA estimates, 95 percent of dioxin intake for a typical person comes from the consumption of animal fats (EPA, 2001). Increasing awareness of the widespread use of elemental chlorine bleaching in pulp and paper production led feminist and environmental activists to question whether disposable products such as diapers, paper towels, coffee filters, menstrual pads, and tampons contain dioxin. Diapers, menstrual and incontinence pads, and tampons are made, in part, from fleecy and absorbent pulp derived from wood cellulose. The fibers are produced through a chemical bleaching process designed to dissolve lignin, the "glue" that holds the cellulose fibers of natural wood together (Armstrong and Scott, 1992; EPA, 1997). These cellulose fibers are the basis of viscose rayon, a major ingredient in most tampons manufactured in the United States and valued for its absorbency.

The cellulose must be separated from the lignin in a process known in the industry as "pulping." Pulping processes are either chemical, mechanical, or semichemical; chemical, or kraft, processing is most common. The wood is cooked with chemicals to dissolve the lignin, then bleached to remove the color associated with residual lignin. There are three general bleaching processes in the US pulping industry: elemental chlorine bleaching, which uses chlorine and hypochlorite and produces chloroform, dioxins, and furans as by-products; elemental chlorine-free bleaching, which uses chlorine dioxide instead of chlorine and no hypochlorite and produces lower levels of chlorinated pollutants; and totally chlorine-free bleaching, which uses oxygen and peroxide or other nonchlorinated agents. Totally chlorine-free bleaching does not produce chlorinated waste products, although all three bleaching processes use large amounts of water and generate substantial quantities of liquid waste (EPA, 1997).

Menstrual and Antitampon Activism

England's WEN launched their Tampon Safety Campaign in England in the summer of 1990, at first focusing on TSS. The Tampon Safety Campaign was soon linked with their Campaign for Unbleached Paper. The campaigns included informative posters and a television documentary about chlorine bleaching of pulp used in feminine hygiene products and disposable diapers. When the half-hour program aired, the television station switchboard was jammed with calls from viewers seeking more information. WEN received thousands of letters inquiring about chlorine and wood pulp. Within just a few months, the major tampon and diaper manufacturers in Britain announced they were switching to chlorine-free methods of bleaching (Armstrong and Scott, 1992).

By the mid-1990s, tampon manufacturers in the United States also switched from elemental chlorine bleaching to chlorine dioxide bleaching of the pulp used in tampons, diapers, and other disposable paper products. Chlorine dioxide, however, can still generate dioxins, albeit at lower levels than elemental chlorine. The Worldwatch Institute calls this switch "a low-tar cigarette approach to the problem of organochlorine pollution," reducing but not eliminating pollution and possible health risks of dioxin in paper products (cited in Bogo, 2001: 1).

Antitampon campaigns in the United States have not been as successful or as visible. Here, the strongest support for antitampon campaigns comes from young feminists and environmental groups, or those who are affiliated with both. Chris Bobel (2003), who has done extensive ethnographic studies of these activists, defines menstrual activism as "various strategic attempts to expose the hazards of commercial 'feminine protection' to both women's bodies and the environment and the promotion of healthier, less expensive and less resource-intensive alternatives" (p. 9). Bobel sees menstrual activism as an outgrowth of the feminist health movement of the 1970s, updated and informed by the D.I.Y. ("Do It Yourself") ethic of the late-twentieth-century punk movement and emerging third-wave feminism.

Among the most visible of such groups is the Student Environmental Action Coalition (SEAC). Dating back to 1996, Tampaction is one of SEAC's oldest campaigns. It began with the College of Wooster chapter and developed into a nationwide campaign, with a website, a clearinghouse, and members who conduct workshops at campuses around the country (gypsy, 2003). After a period of inactivity and false starts, Tampaction has recently reorganized and published an action packet for students interested in starting a campaign on their campuses. At fifty pages, the Tampaction Action Packet provides detailed steps for organizing a campaign, plus description of the campaign and several appendices. As the introduction states, "[t]his is a comprehensive guide to educating yourself and your community about menstrual health, as well as a guide to taking apart an industry that has profited off the shame and degradation of menstruators for decades" (Douglass and Zaidan, 2004: 2).

Although "taking apart an industry" is a bit of exaggeration, the guide is comprehensive. It describes the history of the campaign and provides background on menstrual taboos and product alternatives as well as organizing strategies. It is designed to be a practical, hands-on manual and, accordingly, includes materials that can be easily adapted to the students' specific campuses: "And after all, part of the joy of this campaign is that you are planning it out, implementing your ideas, and getting to see all the happy, healthy bleeders, running around campus thanking and hugging you for liberating them from the mighty tampon oppressors" (Douglass and Zaidan, 2004: 9).

The document is written with a balance of humor and pragmatism, as well as caution to avoid offense. The writers are careful not to equate "menstruators" with women, acknowledging that transgendered, transsexual, genderqueer, and intersexed individuals may or may not menstruate and may or may not identify as women. They also caution organizers not to perpetuate racism, sexism, classism, or homophobia in their campaigns. For example, they do not recommend focusing campaigns on completely removing conventional tampons and pads from school bookstores, as they are aware that the organic disposable products are much more expensive and may therefore be inaccessible to some members of their communities. They recognize, too, that although reusable menstrual items such as cloth pads are cheaper in the long run, it is difficult to persuade others to use them. Douglass and Zaidan (2004) also recommend incorporating anti-oppression work into the campaign, because "[i]f you don't, racism, classism, sexism, and heterosexism will get in the way of effective organizing and will hurt your group" (p. 12).

The Tampaction Action Packet is more carefully developed and user-friendly than some earlier documents, such as the essay about Tampaction that appeared in a 2003 issue of *Threshold,* SEAC's monthly magazine. That article, signed only "gypsy," included the following explanation of why Tampaction opposes tampon use:

> There are many reasons why tampons are dangerous evil things: they are bleached using chemicals, which produce trace amounts of dioxin (a carcinogen). Since dioxin bioaccumulates this is left in wimmin's [sic] bodies and contributes to all sorts of health problems. The reasons tampons are bleached is because in the white supremacist culture of the United States, white is seen as pure and good, anything less than white, even if it's healthier, is considered "dangerous" and "dirty." Most tampons are made of a blend of cotton and rayon. Cotton is a cash crop and regulated by the government as such and not even according to the lax standards our food is held to. This means that pesticides, herbicides, and other killing-cides are in the tampons wimmin [sic] stick up their yonis [sic] every day. (gypsy, 2003: 6)

While it is accurate to describe dioxin as a carcinogen and it is also true that dioxin bioaccumulates, some of these assertions about tampon manufacturing are subject to dispute. More importantly for its purpose, some of this language may alienate potential activists. *Threshold* is a magazine for members of SEAC, so presumably its readers already have an activist bent, although they may not share gypsy's feminist sensibilities. Her apparent choice to align antitampon activism with a woman-centered cultural feminism by use of terms such as *wimmin* and *yoni* may unintentionally disaffect other supporters. Similarly, the rhetorical strategy of aligning SEAC's anti-tampon campaign with antiracist movements may distract readers and potential activists from the focus on tampon safety and environmental issues. Although some might debate the extent to which the United States is a white supremacist culture, to assert that racism is why tampons are white is extremist and inflammatory. Tampons are white because the wood pulp that rayon is derived from is bleached by the chemical process intended to separate the lignin from the cellulose fibers and soften the resulting fiber. The whiteness of menstrual products (and other disposable paper products such as diapers and coffee filters), though valued, is a collateral effect rather than the purpose of bleaching. The femcare industry, however, is guilty of exploiting the pristine whiteness of disposable products to foster the illusion of purity, sterility, and cleanliness.[1]

The *Threshold* article also notes that cotton, one of the ingredients in tampons, is "a cash crop and regulated by the government as such and not even according to the lax standards our food is held to." All agricultural products grown and sold in the United States are cash crops and subject to federal regulation. The bigger problem is that there are no federal standards to regulate the quantities of dioxin or pesticides in femcare products, although there are regulations for other paper products, such as toilet tissue (Lindsey, 1993). The FDA does not implement anywhere near the full level of their authority to regulate tampons, for reasons of both funding and political constraints (Rome and Wolhandler, 1991).

Rayon, the major absorbent ingredient in most tampons, "is evil, too," according to gypsy, in part because "those tiny little fibers in rayon can cut up the inside of your vagina making little lacerations which makes you bleed more." While microscopic fibers from tampons can remain in the vagina after tampons are removed, the health danger posed by these fibers is that tiny ulcerations can become entry points for *Staphylococcus* bacteria. Theoretically, it is also possible for these microscopic particles of viscose rayon to use these vaginal ulcers to enter the lymph system and induce problems elsewhere in the body (Rome and Wolhandler, 1991). Some researchers believe that rayon, like the discredited synthetics of the late 1970s, may provide a hospitable host environment for the TSS bacteria (Tierno, 2001), but the minuscule quantity of blood produced by these microscopic lacerations is unlikely to be perceptible to the menstruating woman.

Environmentalist and activist magazines, such as *E Magazine, Vegetarian Times, Ms., Utne Reader,* and the NWHN newsletter, address tampon safety more frequently than mainstream media. Writers in these fora make reference to sources like the FDA, the IARC, and congressional subcommittees to support their assertions of dioxin's danger, nearly always in milder language than SEAC activists.

For example, *E Magazine*'s piece on the femcare industry offers specific reasons to avoid tampons: the possibility that dioxin remains in the products even after the switch to elemental chlorine-free bleaching; the excessive use of energy, water, and materials in production; the risk of TSS; and the pollution and environmental damage caused by tampon and pad packaging, including tampon applicators (Bogo, 2001). According to the article, more than 170,000 tampon applicators can be found along US coasts in just a single year. During the 1990s, articles with similar arguments appeared in *Buzzworm,* a Canadian environmental journal, and twice in *E Magazine* (Ikramuddin, 1997; Lindsey, 1993).

In 2001, *Utne Reader* offered a broad but brief overview of the controversy, quoting experts such as Dr. Philip Tierno, the NYU microbiologist who opposes trends toward more absorbent tampons with more synthetic materials, and Dr. Jay Gooch, senior scientist for Procter & Gamble, who defends the safety of Tambrands products. In this piece, author Andy Steiner's primary focus is controversy over new, high-absorbency tampons that Procter & Gamble intends to introduce to the US market. These tampons will be labeled "ultra" and positioned as one step above "super plus," the most absorbent tampons currently available here. Ultra tampons will be capable of absorbing 15 to 18 grams of fluid, which Tierno and others believe will increase a woman's risk of developing TSS. However, Gooch points out that ultra tampons are already available in Canada and other markets. Amy Allina of the National Women's Health Network affirms that the introduction of more absorbent tampons was a direct response to consumer demand. She expresses concerns, however, that tampon manufacturers in other countries will not be held to the same regulatory standards as those in the United States (Steiner, 2001).

Tampon safety issues have not been completely ignored by the mainstream press; in fact, it is arguably Karen Houppert's frequently referenced *Village Voice* article, published in 1995, that gave new momentum to student and feminist campaigns in the United States. Frustrated by the increasing price of a box of tampons—while the number of tampons in each box decreased—Houppert put her journalistic skills to work investigating the tampon industry. She criticized the use of shame and secrecy in advertising of menstrual products and questioned the FDA and manufacturer reports that tampons are free of dioxins, citing EPA studies and paper industry reports (Houppert, 1995). The article was widely read and further developed into Houppert's 1999 book, *The Curse: Confronting the Last Unmentionable Taboo: Menstruation.*

Other mainstream coverage includes pieces in the *Worcester Telegram & Gazette* in 1999 about congressional interest in public hearings about dioxin, and Melissa Knopper's extended series with the same focus in the *Chicago Tribune* in 2003. This coverage appears to be sparked by US Representative Carolyn Maloney's (D-NY) proposed tampon safety legislation.

Maloney first became aware of tampon safety concerns several years earlier, when a young constituent working on a project for a college class asked her if tampons were safe. Maloney did not know the answer and began to investigate. She discovered that there is very little research conducted on tampon safety in the United States, and nearly all of it is done by tampon manufacturers. As with most consumer products, the FDA does not commission independent research but relies on data provided by the industry. Maloney responded to her discovery by drafting and introducing the Tampon Safety and Research Act in 1997 (Knopper, 2003). The bill would require independent research on tampon safety under the auspices of the NIH to determine whether dioxins, synthetic fibers, and other additives are present in femcare products and to assess their health risks. The bill was introduced in 1997 and in 1999 but never got out of subcommittee. In 2001, it was renamed "The Robin Danielson Act," after a woman who died of tampon-related TSS in 1998, in hopes that removing the word *tampon* from the title might speed its progress (Knopper, 2003; Maloney, 2003; US House, 2001). The bill was introduced again in early 2003 and quickly moved to the House Subcommittee on Health, but the only action to date has been the addition of a few more cosponsors.

Numerous representatives of antitampon campaigns can be found on the World Wide Web. One much-linked site is "Ruth's Endometriosis Page," created by a Wisconsin woman who suffers from endometriosis, which she believes is linked to dioxins in both the environment and the tampons she used as a teenager. Ruth says she is "not a scientist or a doctor. Just a woman with an attitude and a cause" (Ruth B., 2003). Ruth maintains a large website with links and information about endometriosis, environmental pollution, fibromyalgia, and tampon safety. The tampon information includes the results of independent tests Ruth commissioned on Playtex superabsorbent tampons, which found dioxins and furans in the tampons. When Ruth's story was covered by the Roseville, California, *Press-Tribune* in 1998, the paper had EPA toxicologist Mike DeVito examine the results. He confirmed that Ruth's tested tampons contained between 0.6 and 0.7 picograms of dioxin. DeVito estimates that this would lead to 3.5 percent of a menstruating woman's daily dioxin exposure; averaged over a month's time, "her exposure from tampons would decrease to .93 percent" (Yanello, 1998). Given dioxin's long half-life, however, this exposure would accumulate over time, and the long-term health risks remain unknown.

Ruth is careful, as are most scientists, to point out that women are exposed to far more dioxin through their dietary intake than through tampon use. She remains convinced of a link between dioxin and endometriosis while she awaits further research on the role of tampons in the connection. Ruth's language is characterized by a combination of confidence and the self-effacement strategies of some young feminists described by Chris Bobel (2003). She emphasizes that science is not her area of training or expertise ("just a woman . . ."), but she is sure of what she knows. She responds promptly to reader queries on her message board, often with citations and hyperlinks to further information.

There are several feminist websites devoted exclusively to menstrual health and tampon safety. The sites usually combine interests in the potential health risks of tampon use, environmental concerns with respect to disposable menstrual products, and the corporate focus on profit at the exclusion of women's health and environmental issues, varying in degree and relative priority. A few of the most frequently linked sites are discussed here.[2]

"S.P.O.T. the Tampon Health Website" is linked from personal home pages of young women, the Museum of Menstruation website, the CWHN site, Pandora Pads, and others. Tracy Bannett, the site's creator, was inspired to publish the site in 1995 after reading Houppert's *Village Voice* article. Tracy identifies five main issues with respect to tampon use and safety, each bulleted with a small icon of a circled tampon with a line through it:

- Nearly all major brand tampons contain synthetic fibers.
- Studies have found that Rayon [sic], the synthetic fiber contained in commercial tampons, creates an ideal environment for the growth of the *Staphylococcus aureus* bacteria, which causes Toxic Shock Syndrome.
- Major brand tampons are made of conventionally grown cotton which can be exposed to synthetic fertilizers, herbicides, pesticides and defoliants.
- Plastic tampon applicators from sewage outfalls are one of the most common forms of trash on beaches.
- In my opinion, Tampax and Playtex could care less [sic] about our health—they care more about our money. They keep raising the prices and lowering the number of tampons in a box. (Bannett, 1995)

The rest of the site consists of Tracy's Frequently Asked Questions file, hyperlinks to articles about tampon safety, contact information for alternative product merchandisers, and visitor comments. Tracy is careful to preface her objections to tampons with the phrase, "in my opinion," and encourages her readers to do their own research and analysis. Like Ruth B., Tracy is sure of herself, but her rhetorical choices do not compel the reader to agree. For example, she advises readers to "[e]xplore the site, read articles written by others, look at the alternatives and then make up your own mind. If you feel inspired, stop buying tampons from corporate giants [and] buy organically made products instead." The tone of this message, expressed in phrases such as "if you feel inspired" and "make up your own mind" suggests Tracy doesn't care if you agree with her or not. However, this approach is consistent with the feminist principles of autonomy and informed choice. Tracy doesn't tell her readers what to do but provides information for them to decide for themselves.

The Montreal-based Blood Sisters Project, founded in 1995, is "concerned with the serious health, environmental and psychological ramifications of the toxic feminine hygiene industry and [is] fighting to stop the whitewash on all fronts" (Blood Sisters, n.d.). The group and its website emerged from a "guerilla girl recyclable pad distribution network" and is involved in numerous varieties of menstrual activism, including publishing zines, "terrorizing bathroom walls, giving healthy health workshops, organizing art exhibits, [and] distributing affordable alternative products," always "with winged power" (Blood Sisters, n.d.).

The Blood Sisters page on health, environmental, and social impacts of the tampon industry—aka "What Every Menstruating Woman Needs to Know"—prioritizes the ecological damage of tampon production and use. They cite the chlorine bleaching of paper products as well as the overpackaging of feminine hygiene products. They also address the health risks of dioxin, noting its "probable" association with endometriosis and "possible" link to cervical cancer. They attribute their data to "Stop the Whitewash Campaign" of the WEED (Woman's Environment and Education Development) Foundation (Blood Sisters, n.d.). The WEED Foundation is now known as WHEN, Women's Healthy Environments Network, however, which suggests that the Blood Sisters have not updated their materials recently. As a volunteer-run, nonprofit organization, finding sufficient time and resources to do so is always a challenge (Chris Bobel, February 2004, personal communication).

The Blood Sisters promote direct action, such as writing letters to tampon manufacturers and calling the toll-free numbers on the packages to express concerns about tampon safety. They also recommend writing letters to appropriate government representatives to request stricter control over menstrual products and talking to other women about the issues. The most direct action recommended is to change one's own menstrual practices, by switching to more environmentally and economically sound products, such as reusable cloth pads, sea sponges, or The Keeper (a reusable menstrual cup) (Blood Sisters, n.d.).

Along with hyperlinks and information about numerous other feminist issues, the Lewis & Clark College Womyn's [sic] Center created a Web page in 2001 with information about menstruation and tampon safety campaigns. The page includes a list of the "Top 10 Things To Know About Menstruation," written by Michelle A. L. Singer (2001):

1. Knowledge is power.
2. There are serious health issues related to menstrual products.
3. Media-created perceptions about menstruation do not serve women.
4. One woman will throw away 10,000 disposable pads or tampons in her life.
5. Your menstrual pain is telling you something important.
6. Since there was menstruation, there was respect.
7. You have choices beyond disposable pads and tampons.
8. It feels good to celebrate (aka it doesn't have to be a curse).
9. The menstrual cycle is connected to the cycles of the moon.
10. Remember the way you were introduced to menstruation? Don't pass it on!

Each item includes more detailed information; the focus is on self-knowledge and understanding and developing a positive attitude toward menstruation. The "menstruation" page includes hyperlinks to other menstruation websites, primarily antitampon campaign pages and retail sites for alternative menstrual products, and a reading list of print sources (Lewis & Clark College Womyn's Center, 2001). The Womyn's Center's menstrual activism appears to be part of a third-wave feminist activism more generally. The website also includes links to similar pages on feminism, sexual violence, nutrition, women's health, body image, technology, pro-choice issues, and other feminist topics. (See Bobel [2003] for elaboration on the relationship between menstrual activism and third-wave feminism.)

The Lewis & Clark Womyn's Center also produced a print brochure that includes information derived from Houppert's *Village Voice* article, a *Vegetarian Times* piece by Leora Tanenbaum, Armstrong and Scott's book, and several websites, including some I have reviewed here. The brochure is titled "It's Time To Pull the Plug: A Few Good Reasons Not To Use Tampons" and makes liberal use of graphic images from antitampon websites. (My favorite is the slogan, "Friends don't let friends use tampons," borrowed from Miki Walsh's now-defunct Random Girl website.)

Corporate Responses

These debates and protests have clearly caught the attention of the four major tampon manufacturers in the United States. Although none directly engages the protestors in their public communication, most acknowledge consumer fears and anxieties in their promotional and informational materials. The websites of the four major tampon manufacturers in the United States—Procter & Gamble (Tampax), Playtex, Kotex, and Johnson & Johnson (o.b.)—all feature links to the same FDA consumer information site, "Tampons and Asbestos, Dioxin, & Toxic Shock Syndrome."

The FDA site was published in 1999, in direct response to the Internet rumors of asbestos in tampons. The FDA assures consumers that asbestos is not an ingredient in any US brand of tampon and has never been associated with the fibers used in making tampons. The site also addresses dioxin and rayon concerns: "There are also allegations that some tampons contain toxic amounts of the chemical dioxin" (FDA, 1999). No source of these allegations is identified. Dioxin is briefly defined, then the FDA asserts that "state-of-the-art testing of tampons and tampon materials that can detect even trace amounts of dioxin has shown that dioxin levels are at or below the detectable limit. No risk to health would be expected from these trace amounts" (FDA, 1999). The FDA does not, however, conduct tests of tampons and, in fact, tests very few of the products it approves. As noted above, the FDA relies on testing and reports from the industry, as it does with most consumer products.

These assertions of tampon safety are carefully worded: Dioxins are "at or below the detectable limit" is a different assertion than "dioxins are not present." "No risk to health would be expected from these trace amounts" is a cautious way of saying that the health risks of dioxin in tampons are unknown; the conditional tense of the verb essentially says, "while we don't believe there are health risks, we really don't know."

The site takes the same tone in addressing toxic shock syndrome. This third section of the site begins with the unattributed accusation, "There are also allegations that rayon in tampons causes TSS, and dryness or ulcerations of vaginal tissues" (FDA, 1999). These allegations are neither denied nor confirmed by the statement "vaginal dryness and ulcerations may occur when women use tampons more absorbent than needed for the amount of their menstrual flow" (FDA, 1999). It is recommended that women use tampons of the minimum absorbency required to control their menstrual flow and use the FDA required guidelines to make that assessment.

Of the four companies' consumer websites, Kotex and Tampax provide the most information about tampon safety.[3] The Playtex site contains only a brief—fewer than 100 words—description of TSS and associated risks, with a link to the FDA site. The o.b. site contains no tampon safety information, although users are advised to "please read the package insert for other important information" before using o.b. products.

Tampax maintains a large and detailed website, with information about its products, links to women's health information, and five different tampon question pages. The "Tampon Questions: Tampons Myths and Misconceptions" page addresses the questions of rayon, dioxin, chlorine bleaching, and asbestos before the typical questions about stuck tampons, tampons falling out, and whether or not to bathe during menstruation.

- Is rayon safe to use in tampons?
- Do Tampax tampons contain dioxin?
- Why is bleaching done on the raw materials used to make Tampax tampons? Is it done only to whiten the fibers?
- Do Tampax tampons contain asbestos?
- Can tampons cause endometriosis or cancer?

The answers are yes, no, to eliminate impurities, absolutely not, and no. Like the FDA consumer information page, there is no indication of who raised these questions or how frequently they are asked. Acknowledging how frequently these questions are asked might give unwanted credence to antitampon activists. The seriousness of the questions and implied critique are minimized by being included in a list that includes questions about tampons lost in the body, what to do if the string breaks, and the hoary old chestnut about whether one should wash her hair during menstruation.[4] The questions are answered briefly, authoritatively, and with little detail or support, as if to discourage further questions.

The Kotex site also includes questions about dioxin, rayon, asbestos, and TSS among questions about tampons and virginity, how often to change a pad, and where to find coupons and free samples. Answers to tampon safety questions on the Kotex website frequently include references to research studies; for example, in assuring users that rayon tampons are just as safe as cotton tampons, the site reports that "clinical studies have demonstrated that tampons with rayon and cotton are safe for their intended use, and both rayon and cotton have been used safely in tampons for many years." This was confirmed, according to the site, by "several well-respected research scientists" with affiliations to Dartmouth-Hitchcock Medical Center and the University of Minnesota. Mentioning the universities where research was conducted without citing studies or scientists gives the illusion of specificity in Kotex's responses to tampon safety questions. This strategy lets Kotex attach the ethos of respected research centers without providing any actual evidence.

Interestingly, the Kotex site also addresses environmental concerns, although without labeling them as such. For example, listed questions include "Why are plastic applicators used with Kotex Security tampons?" and "Why are your feminine pads and tampons individually wrapped?" Kotex answers both questions by stating that their research shows repeatedly that women prefer plastic applicators and individually wrapped products. The fact that Kotex must address this issue in the FAQ list, however, suggests that not everyone is enamored of all the extra plastic that comes with their products.[5]

These consumer preferences are easily explained by cultural norms of menstrual shame and secrecy. Individually wrapped products are easier to conceal; a small, pink plastic square containing a folded pad can be easily slipped into a coat pocket or dropped into a book bag or briefcase. An individually wrapped tampon with applicator takes up only slightly more space than a lipstick and is easily concealed in a pocket or purse.

This discretion is often highlighted in advertising for menstrual products, as discussed in Chapter 2. For example, the Tampax "Compak" model's selling point is that it cannot be seen in a closed fist. The only difference between the "Compak" and other tampons with plastic applicators is that the telescoping applicator tubes are already compressed; the user must extend the smaller, internal tube before using the product. This design requires more time and attention from the user to insert, somewhat decreasing its practical convenience. The only plausible advantage to this design is that it can be more easily concealed and carried.

Of course, tampons themselves are actually quite small; it's the applicator preferred by US consumers that increases the size, bulk, and waste of tampons. According to one manufacturer of organic cotton tampons, in the United States only 3 to 4 percent of women use tampons without applicators (sometimes referred to as "digital tampons"), while more than 97 percent of European women prefer them (Organic Essentials, 2003). Of the four major tampon manufacturers in the United States, only one—Johnson & Johnson's o.b.—is available applicator-free. I suspect the US preference for tampons with applicators (like the preference for disposable rather than reusable products) is tied to the shame and stigma associated with menstruation in US culture. Using applicator-free tampons requires a woman to touch her vulva frequently, and may even occasionally cause her to touch her own menstrual blood. These demands are hard to reconcile with the pervasive cultural messages that menstruation is a dirty, contaminating force. Social science research directly exploring this connection between product preferences and attitudes toward menstruation is not yet available.

In the second half of the twentieth century, innovations in menstrual product design are those that make the products less visible, rather than safer or more effective. Menstrual products are sold based on their ability to keep menstruation secret and thus reduce embarrassment. In a climate in which there is little other public communication about menstruation, concerns about tampon safety are difficult for many to address. They're also unprofitable.

Making Tampons Safer

Based on my examination of these discourses to date, I believe that both tampon manufacturers and antitampon activists are presenting claims that are incomplete and thus inaccurate and misleading. For example, manufacturers proudly claim to have switched to elemental chlorine-free bleaching processes, but unless their wood-pulping plants are using oxygen and peroxide or other nonchlorinated agents—and few in the United States are—tampons containing rayon do contain dioxins, albeit in very tiny amounts. "Elemental chlorine free" usually means using chlorine dioxide instead of chlorine and no hypochlorite, which does produce lower levels of chlorinated pollutants, but, as noted earlier, it's more comparable to switching to low-tar cigarettes than to quitting smoking.

Given the pervasiveness of dioxins in the environment, all-cotton tampons are also likely to contain dioxin, regardless of the bleaching method. DeVito and Schecter's (2002) comparative analysis of four different brands of tampons (including both rayon/pulp tampons and all-cotton brands) found trace concentrations in all four, although none contained the most potent dioxins, TCDD and 1,2,3,7,8-penta-chlorodibenzo-*p*-dioxin.

Some activists claim that tampons are bleached to make them white because consumers demand snow-white menstrual products. Tampons are white as a side effect of the chemical process that separates and softens the fibers. Some activists like to say that we don't need tampons to be white, as they are not sterile. We may not need tampons to be white, but we do need them to be soft.

Also, my review of the scientific data presented by both activists and manufacturers indicates that focusing tampon safety debates on the presence of dioxin is misguided. It is clear that dioxins are present in US-manufactured tampons, whether cotton, rayon, or rayon/cotton blends, albeit in minuscule amounts. *What remains to be seen, and should be studied and discussed, is what level of health threat is posed by the presence of dioxin in tampons.*

In a study funded by the International Nonwovens and Disposables Association, Scialli (2001) also found minute quantities of dioxins in both rayon and unbleached cotton tampons; however, he noted that this amount is *at least six orders of magnitude lower* than estimated daily dietary exposure to these contaminants. It is also still unknown how much of the available dioxin in tampons is absorbed vaginally, although it is generally known that most chemicals are absorbed more readily through mucous membranes than through digestion (e.g., sublingual nitroglycerine tablets, rather than pills, are prescribed for heart patients because the medicine enters the bloodstream faster; some migraine drugs are available as nasal sprays for the same reason). EPA researchers have asserted that there is no safe level of dioxin.

Based on their screenings of tampons for dioxins, DeVito and Schecter (2002) argue that it is unlikely that menstrual products contribute in any significant way to a woman's lifetime exposure to dioxins. Even allowing for the possibility that the dioxin content of a typical tampon is absorbed during normal use, dietary exposure dwarfs tampon exposure. They also note that human blood, while not the sole component of menstrual fluid, contains approximately 0.12–0.24 picograms of dioxin per gram—one to fifteen times the concentration in tampons (DeVito and Schecter, 2002).

In the current cultural climate, there appear to be two avenues of productive direct action for tampon safety. One is Representative Maloney's proposed tampon safety legislation, introduced into Congress for the third time early in 2003. If passed, the "Robin Danielson Act" will require the NIH to conduct research

> to determine the extent to which the presence of dioxin, synthetic fibers, and other additives in tampons and other feminine hygiene products (A) poses any risks to the health of women who use the products, including risks relating to cervical cancer, endometriosis, infertility, ovarian cancer, breast cancer, immune system deficiencies, pelvic inflammatory disease, and toxic shock syndrome and (B) poses any risks to the health of children of women who used such products during or before the pregnancies involved, including risks relating to fetal and childhood development. (US House, 2003)

The bill also states that this research shall confirm (or refute) the data submitted by tampon manufacturers to the FDA (US House, 2003). However, the bill does not offer a means of funding or implementing this research program.

The other direct action is for women to stop buying and using these products until and unless their safety is confirmed by reliable third parties.

Alternative Menstrual Products

One measure of the success of menstrual activism and antitampon activism is the increasing availability of alternative menstrual products. These alternatives may not be at your neighborhood drugstore or nearby Wal-Mart, but organic cotton tampons with and without applicators, sea sponges, The Keeper, and reusable cloth pads are readily available at health food stores, some large drugstore chains, and through Internet merchants.

Natracare and Organic Essentials tampons and menstrual pads, made from certified organic cotton, are the primary brands that are available in North America. Promotional materials identify these products as certified organic and free of genetically modified cotton and therefore presumably healthier and safer for consumers and the environment.

Less popular and less readily available are sea sponges. Sea sponges are natural sponges (that is, not cellulose kitchen sponges) sold in small sizes as reusable tampons. Sea sponges are regarded by many as healthier than conventional rayon tampons because they are all natural, although FDA tests have found particles of sand, grit, bacteria, yeast, and mold in sea sponges sold for menstrual use. One sample was confirmed to contain *Staphylococcus aureus,* the bacteria which leads to TSS (FDA, 1995). Sea sponges are also less popular because they are difficult to use correctly; they must be dampened to be inserted, and it is difficult for most women to wring out enough water to keep the sponges from leaking during use. Additionally, once a sponge is saturated, it tends to leak, especially when the user sneezes or laughs.

The Keeper is a small cup made from natural rubber that is worn internally to collect menstrual fluid. Users need to remove and empty it only once or twice a day, rather than replace pads or tampons five to seven times daily. The Keeper is reusable and, in fact, normally lasts for at least ten years. There are no known cases of TSS associated with The Keeper, probably because it collects rather than absorbs menstrual fluid. It is also possible that the number of Keeper users is still too small to yield meaningful data for comparison. Women who are allergic to latex cannot use The Keeper; however, a Canadian company began distributing the DivaCup, an equivalent product made from medical-grade silicone, in 2002 (Health Keeper, 2003).

The language and methods used to market these alternative menstrual products are strikingly different from the presentational discourses of conventional products from the "big four" femcare corporations. The most immediate difference is the venues in which the two categories of menstrual products are discussed; alternative products are seldom discussed or advertised in mainstream women's magazines. This is partly because companies such as Eco-Logique, Glad Rags, Organic Essentials, and Many Moons are small, independent companies without the advertising budget of corporations like Procter & Gamble, Johnson & Johnson, and Kimberly-Clarke. These larger corporations are far more likely to enter agreements for long-term advertising of their diverse product lines with high-circulation women's magazines. Given the level of influence and control large advertisers are known to have over most women's magazines (Steinem,

1990), it is also possible that advertising contracts from these advertisers prohibit editorial content about menstrual alternatives.

Most striking is the way menstruation is framed in ads for alternative products. Ads for ecologically sound products do not market secrecy and shame along with the products. There is no mention of freshness and no remedy for tainted femininity. Menstruation is understood to be a fact of life that one must accept, rather than hide or control.

In support of the ideology of freshness typically promoted in advertising for menstrual products (Berg and Block Coutts, 1994; Kane, 1997), the most recent ads emphasize how new technologies will achieve the desired freshness and help the wearer avoid stains. Each company claims their own proprietary technology of menstrual pads: Kotex pads feature LeakLock®, Stayfree are the only pads with Four Wall Protection®, and Always has its absorbent Gel-Core®.

By marked contrast, ads for organic disposables and reusable cloth pads feature persuasive strategies that emphasize the natural, healthful qualities of the product and practical reasons for using them. The opening paragraph on Natracare's site includes such phrases as "all-natural choice," "100% pure organic GMO free cotton," "certified organic," "natural absorbent core," and "biodegradable plastic liner." The rest of the site's main page is a brief history of the company—something not found on the corporate sites. Natracare's "Health Issues" hyperlink takes the reader to brief definitions and descriptions of irritation, pesticides, dioxin, and TSS—issues ignored or explicitly denied on most corporate sites.

The "Organic Tampons" hyperlink provides more information about one of Natracare's products, along with information about the possible presence of dioxin in conventional rayon tampons. No mention is made about the possible presence of dioxin in cotton, although given its environmental prevalence, it is surely there. Small companies work to elevate their products and their reputation, just as large corporations do. Natracare claims responsibility for creating the demand for their products: "Natracare created the demand for all cotton tampons and launched a PR campaign to educate females about the differences between Natracare and other brands that contained rayon and synthetics" (n.d.). Natracare also claims to be the first company to produce all-cotton tampons.

Organic Essentials also highlights the organic cotton of their products, certified by the Texas Department of Agriculture. The ingredients and method of manufacture are among the first things one learns about Organic Essentials tampons:

> When you choose Organic Essentials' tampons, you are making a positive choice for your own health and the health of the environment. Our Organic Cotton Tampons are made without the use of rayon, synthetic chemicals, binders or fillers. We whiten the cotton with hydrogen peroxide instead of chlorine bleach.

This represents a marked contrast from the Tampax website, which obfuscates the methods and ingredients of tampons manufacture.

The Web page for "Sea Pearls" at Pandora Pads also emphasizes the absence of dioxins and synthetic fibers and the environmental and economic advantages of using sponges over tampons: "Sponge tampons are reusable for 6 months or more. You will feel so good knowing you are not polluting the environment (like disposables do)" (Pandora Pads, 2003).

The Keeper is probably the only menstrual product with what might be termed a "fan base." Users of cloth pads may mention it in intimate conversations and encourage friends to use them, but Keeper users are *devoted*. Fans of The Keeper are legion on the Internet. Their testimonials can be found at the sites of Keeper distributors, the virtual Museum of Menstruation, and at personal websites. A LiveJournal user identified only as Ide Cyan once posted her own mock-ups for advertisements for The Keeper and for the DivaCup on her website (the ads are no longer online). One of these ads featured the actor Reese Witherspoon as lawyer Elle Woods (from the *Legally Blonde* movies) proclaiming, "Next to Bruiser, my Keeper is my best friend" and "Every girl should have a Keeper." Another featured Carrie Fisher as Princess/General Leia and the words, "When I have to lead a whole Rebellion, I don't have time to worry about wearing a pad or tampon into battle. I use the DivaCup." Interestingly, these culture-jamming ads resemble typical femcare product ads in their failure to mention explicitly menstruation or periods. However, they get innovation points for featuring celebrity endorsements (albeit unauthorized), rare in menstrual product ads.

Reusable cloth pads are available from numerous makers and distributors, including Many Moons and Lunapads in Canada and Glad Rags and Pandora Pads in the United States. FAQ files on these websites are usually about the products, rather than about menstruation or womanhood in general (although several feature hyperlinks to women's health sites). Ironically, it is the faceless corporate sites that try to present themselves as friends or confidantes to women. Kotex has tried to create a Web presence where women can "learn about everything, talk about anything," such as "your first bra . . . your first

period . . . your first love . . . your first baby . . . your first hot flash"
(Kimberly-Clark, 2003b, ellipses in original). Tampax has a similar
site with comparable themes for teens at BeingGirl.com.

Cloth pad makers and distributors seem surprisingly collegial for
business competitors. Fierce competition might be expected, as the
market for these products is very small and the items last for years,
by design. Instead, the FAQ file on the Lunapads website contains
the following answer to the question "What makes Lunapads different from other washable pads?":

> In our opinion, any washable pad is a good washable pad! This
> question is simply about what makes Lunapads different from most
> other washable pads, differences that may or may not be important
> to you personally. (Lunapads.com, 2003)

Such endorsement of the competition, tepid though it may be, is
unlikely to ever appear on a Tampax or Kotex website! Janet Trena-
man even includes her original pattern for cloth pads at her website
for Many Moons, allowing users to make their own pads rather than
purchase hers. In addition, Many Moons, Pandora Pads, Eco-
Logique, Lunapads, and Glad Rags are all distributors of The Keeper,
Jade and Pearl sea sponges, and organic cotton tampons as well as
their signature pads. These product categories are compared to each
other, rather than to those of competitors.

These sites also frequently address positive attitudes toward
menstruation in an explicit way. Eco-Logique provides information
and recommended resources about the emotional and physiological
aspects of menarche, menstruation, and menopause, as do Glad Rags
and Lunapads. Eco-Logique frames menstruation as a source of
strength and energy for women:

> From menarche to menopause, menstruation can be exciting, scary,
> energizing or a time of turmoil. Learn more about welcoming
> womanhood, going with the flow, and a time of power and wisdom.
> Learn about the cycles of your body. (Eco-Logique.com, 2003)

The substance and the tone of the advice for young women is markedly
different at Kotex.com and at Eco-Logique.com. Eco-Logique encourages young women to get a mirror and discover what their external
genitalia looks like. *The Period Book* is quoted:

> [I]f this seems like a strange thing to do, it's probably because
> we're taught that this is a private area that should be kept covered.

> But that means private from other people, not private from your-self! After all, a boy's genitals are private, too, but no one thinks it's weird when he looks at them. (Karen and Jennifer Gravelle, quoted in Eco-Logique.com, 2003)

Eco-Logique also introduces the term *menarche* and how to pro-nounce it, information missing from the menstrual education of most North American girls.

Kotex's menarche information page identifies the first period as something that is both "cool" and "something you'll have to deal with every month": "Luckily, in the 21st century a period doesn't have to be a big deal. Prepare yourself with *products* . . ." The page also advises girls to get used to dealing with "raging hormones":

> Hormones are POWERFUL. Don't underestimate the power of hor-mone surges over your *emotions*. They can really increase the intensity of your feelings. Have you ever totally lost control over something that's not important? Blame those hormones. (Kimberly-Clark, 2003b, emphases in original)

Kotex advises girls to mistrust their feelings and assume their emo-tions are inauthentic, and to rely on participation in consumerism to deal with being menstruating women.

Of course, purchasing alternative menstrual products is also a consumerist solution, albeit one that is considerably less expensive and more environmentally sound. As the women of Eco-Logique say:

> Alternative, non-disposable menstrual products will not save the world from environmental harm, war, or poverty. They may change your life a little, making your menstrual cycle an easier and more positive expe-rience for you. They will save you money. They will, just a tiny bit, slow down our use of non-renewable resources and pollutants. And they may be another step on your personal path of acting and speaking in the ways that make you feel best. (Eco-Logique.com, 2003)

No, cloth pads and menstrual cups won't save the world. It is often said that revolutions succeed by changing one mind at a time; the menstrual revolution will begin by changing one tampon at a time.

Notes

1. It is interesting to note that unbleached, brown coffee filters and paper towels are widely available in health food stores in the United States,

yet no company markets a brown, unbleached tampon or menstrual pad—or disposable diaper.

2. This analysis is based on the content and structure of the sites as of the summer of 2003. Of the feminist sites discussed in this section, only Ruth's endometriosis page had been updated by the summer of 2005.

3. This analysis is based on the content and structure of the corporate sites as of the summer of 2003. Websites are subject to frequent revision; unsurprisingly, corporate sites are updated more frequently than personal sites, as my discussion indicates.

4. I am indebted to Chris Bobel for this insight (personal communication, February 2004).

5. I am indebted to Mimi Marinucci for this insight (personal communication, October 2004).

7

The Menstrual Counterculture

IN SPITE OF THE PERVASIVE SECRECY, FEAR, AND EMBARRASSMENT surrounding menstruation and its representations, a small but thriving menstrual counterculture exists in the United States. Much of this counterculture exists on or is facilitated through the Internet. In addition to the online menstrual activism and sales of alternative menstrual products documented in the previous chapter, there are two virtual museums of menstruation, numerous websites of menstrual expression, and consumer products such as Vinnie's Tampon Cases and "ditties" tampons seeking mainstream visibility.

A Museum of Menstruation? What Bloody Good Is That?![1]

For a brief time in the late 1990s, Harry Finley's Museum of Menstruation and Women's Health (MUM) was a physical museum housed in the basement of his suburban Maryland home, but it closed to the public in 1998 and MUM now exists only online at mum.org. Finley invites Web surfers to "[D]iscover the rich history of menstruation and women's health on this Web site for the only museum in the world . . . dedicated to menstruation and women's health!" (Finley, 2000a). The site includes pictures of advertisements for menstrual products, as well as scanned and digital images of many menstrual hygiene products, narratives about menstruation and menstrual experience contributed by visitors to the site, and much more. The museum's stated purpose is to be the world's repository for information about, and "showcase" for, menstruation, including as many cultures as possible. This would include collecting and displaying, when possible, stories, customs, and artifacts, and conducting education about menstruation. Menstrual education would take the form of museum tours, visits to schools and other organizations, this Web site, and compact disks and paper publications. (Finley, 2000b)

It is Finley's hope that his collection will eventually find a home of its own. He believes MUM should be in a high-tourist area of a large city, easily accessible to anyone who wants to see it. Finley would also like to remain director of the museum; he reports that some have objected to this, arguing that his B.A. in philosophy and zealous interest are not sufficient credentials. Others object because he is male. Several reviewers have suggested that MUM go to a medical school, but Finley rebuts:

I think that this would guarantee that few people would see it. And besides, menstruation has little to do with medicine, being largely a cultural subject. It's as if a museum of hair styles should be in a medical school; both hair and menstruation have physical origins, but both are largely nonmedical topics. The body is not medicine. Medicine studies the disorders of the body; menstruation is not a disorder. (Finley, 2000b)

I'm inclined to agree with Finley about the cultural nature of menstruation, but I have qualms about his museum. After reviewing the website; visiting MUM on-site in New Carrollton, Maryland; and interviewing Finley, it is my conclusion that while there is much in MUM that is museum-worthy, Finley is a collector, not a curator, and MUM is a private collection, not a museum.

Museums are community storehouses of collective memory. Museums help communities define their identities and connections with the past (Ambrose and Paine, 1993). Although museum professionals may subscribe to narrow definitions from the American Association of Museums (AAM) or the International Council of Museums (ICOM), the term *museum* has broad application and use in everyday life. Museums vary, in size and purpose, from great international museums like the Smithsonian Institution to local museums like the tiny historical museums one often finds in small towns, and from elite research collections to roadside tourist attractions and numerous points in-between. The Internet explosion of the 1990s has led to the proliferation of virtual museums, which range from online highlights from such highly respected public museums as the Smithsonian or Powerhouse, to those with no physical presence, such as the Bad Fads Museum and MUM. (In fact, the ICOM maintains an exhaustive list of virtual museums.) Ambrose and Paine (1993) note that there are any number of ways to classify museums: by category of collections (art, history, science, military, natural history, etc.); management (government, municipal, commercial, university, etc.); area served (national, local, regional); audience served (specialist, educational, general public); and means of exhibition (traditional, open-air, historic house, etc.).

The literature on museums and museology is immense: According to Preziosi (1995), there has been more published on museums in the past decade than in the previous century. Museums have today become increasingly contested spaces. Struggles have erupted over ownership of ancestral artifacts, allegations of obscenity in modern art works, and disagreement about how to display the *Enola Gay* (Levin, 2001). The potential for controversy is perhaps greatest in public museums, in which citizens can claim at least partial ownership. For example, in the late 1970s, curators at the Smithsonian received hundreds of letters objecting to the Institution's acquisition and display of the chairs occupied by television characters Archie and Edith Bunker of *All in the Family* (Hughes, 1997).[2]

My examination of MUM suggests that what counts as a museum may be controversial as well. Burcaw (1983) offers a dozen definitions of *museum,* including that of the AAM, which defines it as "an organized and permanent nonprofit institution, essentially educational or aesthetic in purpose, with professional staff, which owns and utilizes tangible objects, cares for them, and exhibits them to the public on some regular schedule" (p. 10), and the ICOM, "a nonprofit making, permanent institution in the service of society and of its development, and open to the public, which acquires, conserves, researches, communicates and exhibits, for purposes of study, education and enjoyment, material evidence of people and their environment" (ICOM, 2001). A museum that meets these criteria will normally also have a clearly defined mission statement, which explains the museum's base of support, defines its collection, its history, and its collection policies (Edson and Dean, 1996).

In order to be accredited by the AAM, a museum must meet several standards and definitional criteria. These include legal status as a not-for-profit institution; a formally stated educational mission; a full-time, paid professional staff person who has museum knowledge and experience; and a formal and appropriate program of documentation, care, and use of collections. It must also be open to the public at least 1,000 hours a year, have an appropriate annual operating budget, and have accessioned 80 percent of the collection (AAM, 2001).

In addition to its long history of accredited museums, the United States also has a long history of ersatz museums that are nevertheless a vibrant part of our culture. I am using the term *ersatz museum* to refer to a category of museum that falls short of the AAM accreditation guidelines but is more than a classic dime museum. Andrea Dennett (1997) documents the history of the "dime museum," nearly forgotten now, but in the late nineteenth century as popular as movies are today. In the early 1800s, US museums were miscellaneous collections of curiosities, based on the European notion of a "cabinet of wonders" (p. 21), with an educational mission similar to public museums of today. But these museums were also businesses and needed to attract a paying audience to remain open. By mid-century, with P. T. Barnum's American Museum in New York as the prototype, dime museums had incorporated numerous different categories of entertainment, and their educational agendas had largely evaporated. The new agenda was to amuse.

Of course, accreditation or other recognition by museum professionals is not essential to a collection's success. Ersatz museums such as MUM or the highly successful although short-lived Toaster Museum in Seattle fall somewhere on a continuum between accredited public museums of today and the dime museums of 150 years ago. They do not charge admission, and their expressed mission/ agenda is education, although amusement may be a by-product. Both the Toaster Museum and MUM appear to derive their popularity by amusing viewers as much as educating them. Some exhibits at MUM, such as the Halloween costume made from menstrual pads or the dress made from Instead menstrual cups, seem clearly intended to amuse rather than educate.

MUM, as presently configured, is ineligible for AAM's stamp of approval. Under the AAM's definition, although the MUM website does publish a brief mission statement, MUM isn't even a museum. It is not a legally recognized not-for-profit; it has no paid professional staff; its only staff member has rather limited museum knowledge and no museum experience; it no longer presents public exhibits; its methods of display and interpretation are idiosyncratic; it does not appear to have any program of documentation of collections; and it has no apparent system for care, maintenance, and preservation of its collections. MUM also fails to meet AAM's minimal operation criteria: It is no longer open to the public and has no operating budget to speak of. There are no apparent policies or guidelines regarding acquisition; Finley cheerfully accepts whatever menstrual products and ephemera come his way.

Finley's most vocal critic has been Geneva Kachman, the writer/artist/poet who developed the international holiday Menstrual Monday (further detailed below). She presented a paper critiquing the museum at the 2001 meeting of the Society for Menstrual Cycle Research, debated Harry Finley on the television program *Moral Court,* and has published some of her analysis on her own website, The Museum of the Menovulatory Lifetime.

Kachman's biggest objection to MUM is the poor quality of the scholarship about menstruation (Kachman, personal interview, August 9, 2001). She cites the exhibition on menstrual synchrony, the idea that women who share living quarters will synchronize ovulation and menstruation due to pheromones, as an example. MUM's display on the topic showcases Martha McClintock's 1971 paper "Menstrual Suppression and Synchrony" as the definitive word on menstrual synchrony. In a phone interview with me, Kachman discussed Beverly Strassman's more recent research, which suggests that the claim of menstrual synchrony is largely an artifact of statistical errors. Kachman sent a copy of Strassman's 1999 article, and her own summary of other research refuting menstrual synchrony, to Harry Finley and asked that he update the website exhibit. He acknowledged receipt of her materials, but there have been no changes in the exhibit. Finley and MUM do not acknowledge even that there is controversy about menstrual synchrony. Kachman believes that such errors and omissions in the website mislead readers, especially since the site prominently displays endorsements from Lycos, Encyclopaedia Britannica online, The Mining Company, and *The New York Times* (which labeled the site "odd, funny and well-researched" in a review).

My own examination of the MUM website has revealed other errors in scholarship. For example, in the section on menstrual odor (and elsewhere), he attributes the quote "Menstrual blood . . . represents the essence of femininity" to Simone de Beauvoir and seems to take this statement literally. This is a grievous misinterpretation of Beauvoir's remarks, both globally and specifically. As I've noted elsewhere in this work, Beauvoir is well known for her existentialist belief that there is no essence of femininity (or masculinity, for that matter). Her insightful remarks about menstruation in *The Second Sex* dealt with it as socially constructed.

MUM's treatment of menstrual huts, while not strictly speaking erroneous, is another example of weak scholarship. Finley's exhibition on menstrual huts is rather sparse and superficial for a museum that is purported "to be the world's repository for information about, and 'showcase' for, menstruation, including as many cultures as possible" (Finley, 2000a). Given that menstrual huts are the most well-known example of non-Western menstrual traditions in the popular imagination, one might expect a museum of menstruation to have more to say about the purpose of huts than, "By the way, different cultures had different reasons for this segregation, a subject widely discussed in the anthropology of menstruation" (Finley, 1998).

Kachman has also criticized Finley's reluctance to share power; he insists on complete control of the museum and its website (Kachman, personal interview, August 9, 2001). Finley himself is straightforward about this; in an interview with me, he said he has not tried to obtain 501(c)(3) status for MUM (legal status in the United States as a nonprofit, tax-exempt organization) because one of the requirements is that the organization be governed by a board of directors (Finley, personal interview, August 3, 2001). A museum director would serve at the pleasure of the board, and Finley is unwilling to put himself in a position so vulnerable. He is aware that lack of this status makes his museum ineligible for most grant funding and may limit its growth in other ways.

Kachman's other serious criticism of MUM is what she terms the "overbearing presence" of Finley's voice in the museum—a museum, she notes, dedicated to an experience he has never had (Kachman, personal interview, August 9, 2001). It's easy to substantiate this critique as well—Finley's voice is everywhere. He even inserts comments about himself into letters from readers he publishes on the MUM website. Kachman's objection is not that a man is involved, only that there are so few women's voices at MUM.

For many visitors to his ersatz museum and its website, this appears to be a big draw; Finley gets a lot of kudos for being a man with the courage to talk about menstruation. Most of the interviews he's given to the press and others—and there are many—end up being as much about him and why he's interested in menstruation as about the museum and its mission and goals. I even found this to be the case in my conversations with Finley, despite my intentions not to perpetuate that trend.

However, despite the criticisms Geneva Kachman and I have pre-sented, I do not mean to disparage or diminish the *concept* or need for a Museum of Menstruation and Women's Health. Nor am I attacking Harry Finley personally. I have met him and seen his basement museum, and I found him to be earnest and genuine in his interest in menstruation and his passion for his ersatz museum. In her study of collectors and the development of collections, Marjorie Akin (1996) notes that collectors often believe they are preserving something of importance from destruction; in his remarks on the MUM website and in his conversations with me, Harry Finley clearly believes he is doing so.

MUM has already served informally as a clearinghouse and resource for activists and scholars interested in menstruation: It's how Geneva Kachman met Daisy Decapite, who provided illustrations for the first Menstrual Monday posters. MUM has a long- and well-established presence on the Web and is featured prominently in any search engine results on menstruation.

And as Finley points out (personal interview, August 3, 2001), no one else is doing this. The Smithsonian does have a small collection of feminine hygiene items, but they are kept in storage, not on display. Finley says this is why he will not donate his collection to the Smithsonian; he is adamant that his museum must be seen. He claims that the Smithsonian has asked twice for his collection (Finley, 2000b). A curator in the Division of Science, Medicine, and Society at the Smithsonian told me that although she and several colleagues did visit the physical museum site when it first opened, they have never asked him for his collection. She added that they would have no interest in it, as it is mostly facsimiles and reproductions (Katherine Ott, personal interview, August 2, 2001).

Having visited Finley's basement more recently than she, I'm not as certain. Although most of Finley's ads and patent applications are probably copies, he does have a substantial collection of menstrual products that probably are museum-worthy. Many were similar to items I viewed in the Smithsonian's collection, and most were in excellent condition.

There is arguably a strong need for just such a clearinghouse or repository. The last quarter-century has revealed an increased cultural and political interest in menstruation; this book itself is evidence of such interests. I support Finley's assertion that there is indeed a "rich history of menstruation." It is a history that is largely undocumented, and Finley's role in collecting some of that documentation should not be underestimated. The history of menstruation is a history of its concealment and can teach us a great deal about shame, taboo, sexuality, and gender. A public, accredited museum may be an excellent way to do that. Harry Finley's collection and contributions should be included and acknowledged, but MUM is not that museum. Also, in spite of his apparently genuine interest in menstruation and enthusiasm for this project, I am not convinced that Finley is a good candidate to develop this museum. Finley's MUM, however, continues to be a very important hub of the menstrual counterculture.

Another Museum of Menstruation: MOLT

Following her public critiques of Finley's MUM (Kachman, 2000, 2001), Kachman created her own virtual museum. She named it Museum of the Menovulatory Lifetime, with the acronym MOLT. It can be found online at moltx.org. MOLT is not a museum by AAM or ICOM standards either, and it is very different in nature from MUM. It is also considerably smaller, in comparative embryonic stage next to Finley's elaborate website.

MOLT's pages display Kachman's efforts to develop interactive exhibits. For example, her detailed exhibit about menstrual synchrony includes summaries of research, quotes from various experts, and a do-it-yourself experiment with tape measures intended to demonstrate the impossibility of synchrony of menstrual cycles with periods that are noninteger multiples of each other and the apparent synchrony of menstrual cycles whose periods are integer multiples of each other (Kachman, 2002). Essentially, Kachman shows that menstrual synchrony is really menstrual overlap.

Like Finley, Kachman also lacks academic credentials, but she displays herself and MOLT to be in conversation with scholars of menstruation, literally and figuratively. The menstrual synchrony exhibit cites and references appropriate scholarship on menstrual synchrony. Geneva has also presented her own work at the Blood, Body, and Brand Conference about menstruation held at the University of Liverpool in 2003, and at meetings of the Society for Menstrual Cycle Research, of which she was a member until her voluntary withdrawal in 2004 (Harry Finley is also a member).

Kachman comes to the project of a menstruation museum with a clearer statement of interest and mission, developed through her creation of the Menstrual Monday holiday in 2000. Menstrual Monday was founded with a four-part mission statement:

- create a sense of fun around menstruation;
- encourage women to take charge of their menstrual and reproductive health care;
- create greater visibility of menstruation, in film, print, music,
  and other media; and
- enhance honesty about menstruation in our relationships.

Kachman, along with her friends Molly Strange and Janis Hunter-Paulk, first developed and promoted the Menstrual Monday concept in 2000. The idea originated in a parody she had written of Madonna's early 1980s hit "Holiday" with a menstrual theme. The group sent notices to MUM and to menstruation-related listservs and mailed posters and flyers to campus women's groups and anyone else they could think of who might be interested. The materials listed the following suggestions for celebration:

> Wear a red article of clothing, put a red tablecloth on the table at dinner; talk to an older or younger relative about her menstrual experiences; create some art or do some writing about menstrua- tion, and share with friends; share information about PMS, endo- metriosis, or self-breast examinations; create a ritual involving red candles and red tulips. In short: Whatever seems convenient and appropriate to you! (Kachman et al., 2000)

The group also offered a free "starter kit" to help menstruators and celebrants get the party started. That first year, the kit contained a MenstruMobile (a mobile of a cardboard uterus, with cotton ovaries and streaming red ribbons emerging from the cervix; see Figure 7.1);[3] a PMS blow-out (a party horn with a tampon applicator for a tube); menstrumoney (play money with menstrual themes and inspi- rational quotes); a bumper sticker that read, "Honk if you have your period"; tamposes (corsages made from tampons dyed red); instruc- tions for a menstrual meditation; and other items. The response was astonishing. Kachman expected they might receive requests for as many as 100 kits; more than 900 were ordered, by individual women, resident advisors for dorm floors, even by a dad seeking one for his adolescent daughter. Kachman and her friends made all the items themselves and shipped them at their own expense.

The holiday continues to grow and develop, although cost pro- hibits Kachman from creating and sending hundreds of boxes filled with whimsical party favors and celebration ideas. In 2002, Kachman sought corporate sponsorship of Menstrual Monday from Procter & Gamble, makers of Tampax. Their public relations officer reportedly

**Figure 7.1 Geneva Kachman's
MenstruMobile, 2000**

Source: Used with permission of
Geneva Kachman, curator, MOLT: Museum
of the Menovulatory Lifetime.

told Geneva that the holiday was
"too much about menstruation"
(Kachman, personal communication, February 2002). In 2002,
she promoted a contest to develop
alternative menstrual product ads.
The winning entries were displayed in Kachman's presentations
to the Blood, Body, and Brand
Conference at the University of
Liverpool in January 2003 and the
June 2003 meeting of the Society
for Menstrual Cycle Research.

Neither MOLT nor Menstrual
Monday has received the level of
media attention that Harry Finley
has achieved for MUM. However,
extant coverage, mostly on the
Internet and in campus newspapers, focuses on the holiday and
its celebration rather than on
Kachman and her interest in menstruation. Perhaps because she is
female and her own experience of
menstruation clearly and sometimes brazenly informs her poetry,
artwork, and virtual museum
work, attention to her projects can
be more easily focused on the
projects rather than her character.

Of course, MOLT is no more
a museum than MUM under the AAM's definition cited above.
MOLT has a mission statement but is not a legally recognized not-
for-profit and has no paid professional staff. Like MUM, its methods
of display and interpretation are idiosyncratic; indeed, MOLT as yet
has few exhibits or artifacts.

Bringing Menstruation Out of the Closet

Some readers may consider the idea of a museum of menstruation
far-fetched, even outrageous. It is probably difficult for such readers

to imagine the public display of artifacts they've spent much of their lives learning to hide. This challenge to definitions of public and private is precisely why a museum of menstruation offers such powerful educational potential. The categories of "public" and "private" are not natural categories but an artificial framework that is often used to create or reinforce hierarchies. Beauvoir and other feminist theorists have shown how the separation of public and private is used to support a hierarchical sex/gender system, in which women occupy the private realm of home and body, which is usually regarded as complementary and inferior to men's public realm of work and politics. A public, political life is possible only by contrasting it to a domestic, private life.

Keeping menstruation part of that private, domestic life has contributed to its stigma and shame—and to the ignorance about menstruation described in Chapter 5. A museum of menstruation, ideally a multisite public educational institution, could play a significant role in reducing the stigma of menstruation. As noted above, the history of menstruation is largely undocumented, and there is much to learn about menstruation and the technologies of managing it. Schools could arrange field trips to enrich conventional menstruation and sexuality education, and individuals and families could visit anytime.

I do not mean to exaggerate or overestimate the potential educational value of a museum of menstruation, but the popularity of Harry Finley's website has demonstrated that there is a great deal of interest in the artifacts and history of the menstrual products industry. The enthusiasm for Geneva Kachman's Menstrual Monday celebration is also indicative of interest in establishing greater openness and positive attitudes toward menstruation. Finley and Kachman have both made noteworthy and substantial contributions to the movement to bring menstruation out of the water closet, so to speak. Yet it may be the case that neither can bring a real museum to fruition. Perhaps a third party will build on the foundations they have laid, or even develop an alternative medium or venue.

One possibility for an alternative means of making menstruation discourse public is documentary film. Giovanna Chesler's film *Period: The End of Menstruation?* is scheduled for release in late 2005. Chesler believes menstruation is the root of misogyny and brings her critical feminist eye and her camera to the current debates about menstrual suppression. The film presents physicians who promote menstrual suppression and activists who oppose it, school children learning about menstruation in class, a postmenopausal women's group, and an artist who creates paintings with her own menstrual blood, among others talking about menstruation. Although Chesler is explicit in her feminist motives for making the film (Chesler, 2005), within it she "expresses the variety of opinions, facts and figures available on the topic and creates a space for women to make informed decisions about their bodies" (Chesler, 2004). The film has had only limited public screenings as of this writing, making predictions of its possible impact on audiences impracticable.

Menstruation and Style

Although I have framed my analysis in this book as one of public debates and popular culture representations of menstruation, I suspect some readers will consider many of the cultural artifacts and menstrual alternatives I have discussed to be underground rather than public or mainstream. For example, in talks with young women on my campus, I find that few know that alternative menstrual products such as The Keeper or reusable cloth pads even exist. And some readily admit that they find both products to be repulsive, as they cannot imagine handling their own menstrual blood. In such a cultural context, it's difficult to imagine a "popular" menstrual culture.

Yet the possibility looms. New York entrepreneur Vinnie D'Angelo has been working to mainstream menstrual counterculture with Vinnie's Tampon Cases:

> Tired of spending big bucks on tampons only to find them mangled at the bottom of your back pack? Sick of not having a pad when you really need one? Then you need **VINNIE'S TAMPON CASE!!**
>
> Finally, a menstruation product that announces itself with authority! No more euphemisms. No more keeping a tampon in an old sock. Use VINNIE'S TAMPON CASE and be proud of your period! It's natural!!! (D'Angelo, n.d., emphasis in original)

D'Angelo's website, tamponcase.com, is just one of hundreds of places to purchase Vinnie's Tampon Cases. Although today's cases are vinyl, the original Vinnie's Tampon Cases were made of sturdy cotton duck, and they were decorated with cartoon drawings of Vinnie and menstrual puns, such as a cartoon of Vinnie driving a truck and saying, "I brake for cycles" (see Figure 7.2). The cases retail for less than ten dollars each, and are available through numerous specialty shops and online retailers.

Figure 7.2 Vinnie's Tampon Case, 2000

Source: Used with permission of Vinnie D'Angelo.

According to interviews, D'Angelo's motivation in developing his tampon cases was to help out his female friends. He would see them fishing in purses or backpacks for a tampon and retrieve "a mangled applicator and a lump of cotton with old gum stuck to the string" (quoted in Raappana, n.d.). He also liked the idea of changing attitudes toward menstruation. He told Saara Myrene Raappana of the online magazine *Actionman:*

> I get letters every single day and have for years. It just blows my mind that this product hadn't existed before, and now that it exists, ·people really want it. I think that says something about our society . . . that the product filled a void. The idea of putting the words 'tampon case' overtly on the product itself is what endears it to people . . . and the fact that my name is Vinnie somehow makes it that much more powerful—it's a name that's usually associated with the lowest man in our society. You know, Vinnie's the guy who fixes your car, Vinnie's not the guy who's going to be sensitive toward menstrual issues. (quoted in Raappana, n.d.)

Interviews with D'Angelo reveal a feminist sensibility that extends beyond providing menstrual support. In Lori Greenberg's interview with D'Angelo for the "Adios Barbie!" website, he describes a feminist epiphany inspired by hearing his female roommates come home from work with stories about men who harassed them on the street. Said D'Angelo, "That struck a real chord in me."

> It made me realize that women have a very different experience on the planet than men do. In the United States, where there's a big backlash against political correctness and affirmative action, everyone thinks women are equal now and the playing field is leveled. And it's so far from that. (quoted in Greenberg, n.d.)

This feminist consciousness and willingness to use the label *feminist* contrast sharply with Finley's self-defined motivation for creating a museum of menstruation; whereas Finley finds menstruation "interesting," D'Angelo presents his project in terms of improving women's—and men's—lives.

> I love my job.
> I wake up, put on my pants one leg at a time, then my Vinnie's Tampon Case Distributor shirt, wash my face, brush my eyebrows, grab a slice of homemade cold pizza for breakfast, and I'm out the door. The sooner I can be on the street distributing my tampon cases the better. The morning is a great time to pass my personable pouch among the populous [sic]; folks are just waking up, wiping the late nite [sic] TV out of their eyes, and when I hand 'em a Vinnie's Tampon Case they aren't awake enough to remember that they are squeamish about menstruation.
> And there is no need to be squeamish about the natural cycle! Which is precisely what VINNIE'S TAMPON CASE reminds them when they come across it on their desk during lunch in school or at the office. With my smilin' cartoon face looking up at them, they decide then and there—"What the hey! I love my brand new VINNIE'S TAMPON CASE, and I don't care what anyone says!" (quoted in Ratliff and Johnson, n.d.)

While I find much to admire about D'Angelo's attitude and his feminist sensibility, I'm tempted to question the extent to which his enterprise is about liberating women from menstrual oppression. Like Finley, he's a man benefiting from the exploitation of an experience he's never had. Finley has received no financial benefit, only Internet notoriety, but since the introduction of his eponymous tampon case in the late 1990s, D'Angelo has also introduced Vinnie's Giant Roller Coaster Period Chart and Sticker Book, and Vinnie's Cramp Relieving Bubble Bath, packaged with Vinnies' Soothing Bubble Beats CD of "music to menstruate by." D'Angelo is making menstruation hip—and profitable, too.

In my most optimistic moments, I like to think that projects like D'Angelo's empire and Finley's museum take women and men one step closer to the kind of existential reciprocity Beauvoir proposes as the ideal human relationship: "each individual freely recognizes the other, each regarding himself and the other as object and as subject in a reciprocal manner" (1952: 158). But Finley's insistence on complete control and D'Angelo's financial ambitions bring out a more cynical view.

As noted in Chapter 3, media portrayals of men dealing with menstruation typically show men as extremely uncomfortable even talking about menstruation, much less handling menstrual products, making Finley and D'Angelo rare prototypes. One other notable exception, Dave Foley's Kids in the Hall monologue about "the guy with a good attitude towards menstruation," is intended as humor, apparently mocking the sensitive, New Age guy who is comfortable dealing with menstruating women (see Figure 7.3).

I confess to some ambivalence here: I am uncertain about what men's role should be in celebrating menstruation. I appreciate Finley's genuine curiosity, and I admire D'Angelo's feminist approach and his lack of squeamishness. I'm glad to see men talking about menstruation and not insisting that it remain hidden. I like D'Angelo's playful, accepting attitude toward menstruation, but at the same time, I find the fact that he has built a cottage industry of it vaguely exploitive. No one is harmed by his products, of course, but it is more than a little ironic that someone who doesn't menstruate launched this successful line of whimsical, self-conscious menstrual products. On the other hand, perhaps D'Angelo's masculinity adds a social legitimacy (as well as a humorous novelty element, as he noted in the Actionman interview) that a woman's name would not carry in the current cultural climate. And he's great with the clever slogans: He owns the domain name knowyourflow.com, and recent ads for his tampon case say, "Don't let your period cramp your style."

My hesitation in fully endorsing these projects is situated in the larger struggle this book wrestles with over who "owns" menstruation. I favor greater openness and less shame regarding menstruation for both women and men, and I don't consider maleness or masculinity disqualifying characteristics for menstrual activists and educators. Yet I remain uneasy with a menstrual counterculture in which the most visible projects are created and promoted by nonmenstruators. It seems premature in a society in which so few of those who do menstruate are able to safely and freely claim that identity publicly.

Figure 7.3 The Guy with a Good Attitude Toward Menstruation

DAVE: Hi, my name's Dave Foley, and, uh, something you might not know about me is that . . . I have a good attitude towards menstruation. That's right, I'm the guy! The guy with a good attitude towards menstruation!

Oh, I know a lot of men are made uncomfortable by this monthly miracle. But not me. No, I embrace it. Embrace it the way some men embrace the weekend! Why, I anticipate it the way a child anticipates Christmas!

Did you know that, uh, in a lot of native Indian cultures, menstruating women were forced to leave the village, lest their *powerful* magic should overwhelm the Shaman? If I were Shaman, I wouldn't be so competitive. I'd be more open and giving. I'd be a shaman with . . . a good attitude towards menstruation!

'Cause after all, what is it? A cluster of blood vessels, awaiting a fertilized egg. Providing a safe warm place for that egg to grow. And if a life does not occur, the whole thing is flushed away, and the cycle begins again. Now is that anything to be ashamed of or disgusted by? No, this is the nesting stuff of humanity!

That's why the woman I shall love will be able to menstruate as fully and freely as she desires. Even if her monthly flow should build in intensity to a raging rust-colored torrent! An unbridled river of life-giving blood flowing from between her legs! An awesome cataract plunging off the edge of our couch. I wouldn't be fazed! No, no, even if Coureur de Bois would come up stream, battling the rapids, and singing a "jaunty song"! I would take no offense, rather I would ford across that mighty womanly river, and fetch herbal tea and Pamprin. And then I would mop her brow and admire her fecundity. For I . . . Have A Good Attitude . . . Towards MENSTRUATION!

Source: Kids in the Hall/Broadway Video, from Kids in the Hall FAQ. Transcribed by lkane@ix.netcom.com.

However, I'm also ambivalent about the newest entrant in the commercialization-of-menstruation sweepstakes, Dittie tampons. According to their press kit, "Dittie is the first premium brand of feminine protection that is as fun and stylish as it is reliable and trustworthy." The press kit suggests that "you may also be wondering, 'What makes Dittie different from other brands of feminine protection?'" Again, according to the company's press kit,

Dittie looks like something you'd find at the cosmetic counter, not in the pharmaceutical aisle, so you can feel free to flaunt them—in your car, at the counter, by the bathroom sink. And Dittie's not just pretty on the outside. Inside, each individual Dittie features a fun, empowering Dittie message that will make you smile, laugh, think and feel good.

The company's president and developer, Barbara Carey, considers Ditties to be a "lifestyle product." Carey, an entrepreneur with a dozen patents to her name and more pending, developed Ditties with a mission about empowerment and ending menstrual taboo—two laudable feminist goals. But it's also clear that this product encourages a consumer identity, even promotes shopping as a form of self-serving activism. Carey wanted to create "a network of girls and women who are proud to buy, wear and share their Ditties." On the company's website, consumers can download a form to present to the store manager where they shop to demand "I Want My Ditties!" One can also send Dittie-themed e-cards to friends, including a disturbing endorsement of antiwoman stereotypes of premenstrual syndrome that proclaims, "I've got PMS. What's your excuse?" (see Figure 7.4).

The company is not yet profitable, but Carey reported in a telephone conversation that sales are increasing and they've received hundreds of e-mails about the product, mostly favorable. Carey also

Figure 7.4 Dittie PMS E-card, 2004

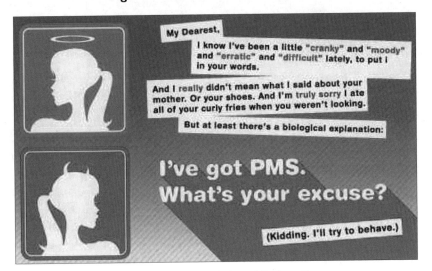

Source: Used with permission of Barbara Carey.

reports that, although the product was designed primarily for teens and young women, 42 percent of Ditties customers are over forty, and half are buying the decorative tampons for themselves (personal interview, September 1, 2005).

As for the sassy sayings, or "mood-lifting messages" as the company prefers to call them, I found a disconcerting mix of fortune-cookie affirmations and unfortunate stereotypes in the box of Dittie tampons I examined:

- "If you're going to wear the pants in the relationship, be sure they're designer."
- "Make every day independence day—pledge allegiance to yourself."
- "PMS means never having to say you're sorry."
- "If you can't be with the one you love, love the one you are."
- "Repeat after me: I do not NEED a man. I WANT a man. (There's a big difference.)"
- "I've got PMS. What's your excuse?"

I did find one slogan I could endorse: "Don't just change your tampon, change the world!"

Ironically, it was printed on a plastic wrapper of a rayon tampon with a plastic applicator. If you really want to change the world, you'll stop using tampons.

Making Menstruation Mainstream— Try Not to Sound Wombmoonly

Most efforts to reframe menstruation and challenge negative attitudes come from explicitly feminist perspectives. Feminist writers tell of discovering ways to celebrate and honor their periods, such as the Bleed-In staged by Janice Delaney, Mary Jane Lupton, and Emily Toth (1988) or the party marking the thirteenth anniversary of one woman's menarche (Culpepper, 1991). These celebrations involved storytelling and reminiscing about menstrual experiences and featured menstrual paraphernalia for decor. Other women have written about acknowledging their periods with quieter celebrations, spending time alone to meditate or relax or take advantage of the extra creativity many women feel at this time (Culpepper, 1991; Francia, 1991; Ouellette, 1991; Owen, 1991). Some make their own cloth menstrual pads and enjoy the ritualistic aspects of using and taking care of them (Taylor, 1988; Owen, 1991). Some women keep special calendars, often lunar, to record their menstrual cycle (Culpepper, 1991). Others simply try to adjust their work schedules to minimize their discomfort (Martin, 1987; Ouellette, 1991).

A few women are also developing special rituals to welcome the menarche of their daughters (Francia, 1991; Delaney, Lupton, and Toth, 1988; Boylan, 2001; Taylor, 1988). Once, daughters in some European and Jewish traditions received a slap in the face upon announcing their first period to their mothers. Now, some daughters are honored with special, women-only celebrations with songs or prayers and candles (Boylan, 2001; Francia, 1991; Taylor, 1988); others are honored by the whole family with a special dinner and a grown-up glass of red wine. Special gifts for the menarcheal girl include calendars and clocks (Delaney, Lupton, and Toth, 1988).

Often, although not always, such attitudes are linked to goddess spirituality. In *The Curse,* Karen Houppert refers somewhat snarkily to such menstrual advocates as Celebrate-Your-Cycle feminists, "goddess feminists with a 1990s twist" (1999: 214). She describes their essentialist feminism as more retreat than resistance. These approaches to menstruation concentrate on connecting with natural cycles and the seasons, emphasizing women's closer connection to nature. Many of the third-wave menstrual activists studied by Chris Bobel (2003) would likely agree with Houppert. Bobel cites such quotes as the following to illustrate this trend and their resistance:

> I'm desperately attempting to not sound really cheesy and womb-moonly, but I think there is a definite value to radical menstruation because it breaks down those sterile walls of individually wrapped plastic devices that keep us from becoming friends with our vaginas. (*It's Your Fucking Body* #2: 6–7, cited in Bobel, 2003)

However, the positions of both the cultural feminists and these young third-wave feminists are foreign and extreme to many women; outside of limited feminist circles, neither menarche nor menstruation are events to celebrate or honor. Although one sometimes hears that menstrual taboos in modern life are fading, empirical research finds the social stigma of menstruation to be thriving (Kowalski and Chapple, 2000; Roberts et al., 2002).

For example, I interviewed teen girls about their menarcheal experiences for a previous project (Kissling, 1996a), and most of the girls found the idea of a menstrual celebration to be laughable or embarrassing. One said, "I wouldn't want to celebrate something that's not very exciting, you know!" Another responded to her sister's suggestion of a simple lunch date and shopping trip with mom with, "No way! I wouldn't do that. I'd say, 'Skip it, Mom!'" I asked the youngest of my informants, who had not yet started menstruating, how she wants her parents to react when she announces her first period. She replied that all she wants is for her mom to provide menstrual supplies: "I would *not* want to celebrate it. Not even a pat on the back."

The enthusiastic interest of US women in menstrual suppression appears to support this research (Fuentes, 2002; Tsao, 2002; see also Chapter 5). Preliminary studies suggest, in fact, that negative attitudes toward menstruation are a better predictor of interest in menstrual suppression than are negative menstrual *symptoms* (Hoyt and Andrist, 2003). In a society in which women are sold pills to suppress their cycles and menstrual products are designed not only to conceal all evidence of menstruation but to be themselves concealed, it's difficult to imagine the menstrual counterculture will supersede the current menstrual culture.

Notes

1. Title suggested by Jenny Thomson (personal communication, October, 2001).

2. The Bunkers' chairs have since become one of the most popular exhibits (Hughes, 1997).

3. Kachman has since renamed the MenstruMobile the U.F.O., or Uterine Flying Object. She now makes them in a variety of colors, including silver in 2005 to commemorate the twenty-fifth anniversary of the tampon and toxic shock syndrome controversy.

8

Conclusion:
How to Break a Curse

WITHIN THE CURRENT CULTURAL LOGIC OF LATE CAPITALISM, A woman's relationship to her menstrual cycle is largely defined through consumer products. Whether this relationship was governed by rhythms of nature in some unspecified ancient past, as some holistic practitioners assert (for example, see Northrup, 1998; Pope, 2001), is immaterial. As John Fiske has noted, contemporary capitalist societies lack a "so-called authentic folk culture" to compare with the perceived inauthenticity of mass culture, making "bemoaning the loss of the authentic a fruitless exercise in romantic nostalgia" (1992: 283).

This consumerist relationship to menstruation has not only become a naturalized way of life, it has come to exemplify what Steven Miles calls "the consuming paradox": "[I]n terms of our individual experience consumerism appears to have a fascinating, arguably fulfilling, personal appeal and yet [it] simultaneously plays some form of ideological role in actually *controlling* the character of everyday life" (1998: 5, emphasis in original).

The commercial exploitation of menstruation is arguably the best thing that ever happened to women—and also the worst. Readily available, relatively inexpensive menstrual management products that are comfortable, effective, and easy to use have permitted women to participate more freely in economic, educational, and leisure activities. Women can work in nearly any occupation, attend school, and play sports more comfortably and more easily than before. Yet, as mobility provided by menstrual products increased, so did the demands of "freshness" required of women. As Chapter 2 details, in the commercial world of so-called feminine hygiene products, menstruation is portrayed as a literal and figurative stain on one's femininity. Women are urged by advertisements to "stay clean, stay fresh, stay free," as if their freedom depends upon their freshness.

The freedom (if not freshness) in women's everyday lives enabled by modern menstrual products is truly transformative, but freedom is never really free, at least under consumer capitalism. To enjoy the liberty granted by products that reduce discomfort, relieve pain, and increase freedom of movement, women must participate in the construction of their own Otherness. In using these products, women are compelled to buy into the idea of the menstruating woman as one of tainted femininity.

The chief mechanism of this process is what Beauvoir (1952) labels mystification. Myths about women and their supposed nature are used to sustain nonreciprocal relations between women and men. The dominant ideologies about women—and about menstruation—are internalized.

I am well aware that such a stance could easily lead to political paralysis. Perhaps such paralysis is also a feature of late capitalism, as Fredric Jameson notes:

> Insofar as the theorist wins, therefore, by constructing an increasingly closed and terrifying machine, to that very degree he [sic] loses, since the critical capacity of his work is thereby paralyzed, and the impulses of negation and revolt, not to speak of those of social transformation, are increasingly perceived as vain and trivial in the face of the model itself. (Jameson, 1984: 57)

But paralysis is not characteristic of feminist critique and activism. Nor is it characteristic of Beauvoir's existentialism. A key tenet of existentialism is that identity is created through activity; that is, one is what one does. "[T]here is no true living reality except as manifested by the conscious individual through activities and in the bosom of a society" (Beauvoir, 1952: 41).

A vivid, dramatic illustration of existentially claiming one's identity as a menstruating woman can be seen in Joan Fern Shaw's (1988) little-known short story "A Period of Quiet but Colorful Protest." Shaw tells the tale of a middle-aged woman who decides to protest the recently increased "luxury tax" on menstrual products *by ceasing to use them.* She simply lets her blood flow, leaving spots on bus seats and a tiny trail of droplets on the floor beneath her as she explains her protest to an observer. Slowly, other women begin to support and join her protest.

However evocative women may find Shaw's story, it is unlikely, to say the least, that such a protest would ever be carried out on a widespread basis in late-capitalist United States, for reasons political, personal, and practical. For most women, choosing to let it flow doesn't even feel like a realistic option. However, postmodern women can let it flow *symbolically*—through their language and communication, as well as their actions and attitudes, about menstruation.

Beauvoir's feminist existentialism recognizes woman's Otherness as situational; to achieve an authentic existence as a Subject, one defines oneself by making choices in the world. With self-awareness and awareness of the conditions of the world in which she lives, a woman can create her own identity and existence, and redefine her relationship to her menstrual cycle. So if our cycles mandate participation in consumer culture, we can use our voices and our dollars to insist that advertisers promote menstrual products on the basis of the merits of the products, instead of cloaking menstruation with shame and secrecy. We can applaud media portrayals of menstruation as empowering, not disabling. As Roseanne advised her TV daughter, we're going to be throwing a lot farther now. We can demand safe and ecologically sound products from manufacturers and from the federal agencies charged with regulating them—and buy or make reusable menstrual pads unless and until they do.

Carolyn Maloney's proposed Tampon Safety Act languishes in committee in part because too many legislators are squeamish about the subject. The bill was renamed The Robin Danielson Act, after a woman who died from TSS, so that it could be referred to without uttering the word *tampon*. If more women and men spoke out about menstruation, legislators might find it harder to remain silent.

We can refuse medication for physiological states that are not diseases. We can display, not hide, the ephemera of menstruation, as playful provocateurs like Geneva Kachman, Vinnie D'Angelo, Barbara Carey, and Harry Finley encourage. Participating in these strategies of resistance—all of them or just one or two—will help to bring the menstrual underground to the surface.

Of course, being loud and proud about menstruation will not solve all of women's problems, nor will it end war and injustice. It will, however, advance gender equality by helping to reduce the secrecy, shame, and stigma associated with menstruation. As Alice Walker (1983) once wrote, "only justice can stop a curse." In this frequently cited essay, Walker was speaking of the need to resist the temptation to surrender to one's cynicism in combating war and oppression. While I recognize that the exploitation of menstruation for corporate profit is not equivalent to the proliferation of nuclear weapons, I believe the same sentiment applies to the "curse" of menstruation.

Menstrual justice will mean that menstruation is no longer each woman's shameful secret, but a fact of life that need not be concealed. Menstruation won't be a curse when women determine how they relate to their menstrual cycles on their own terms. As Beauvoir wrote, it is not menstruation that makes woman the Other. When women can claim authority and authenticity as subjects of their own lives and live as transcendent subjects, menstruation will no longer be woman's curse.

References

Abplanalp, J. M. (1983). "Premenstrual Syndrome: A Selective Review." In S. Golub (ed.), *Lifting the Curse of Menstruation: A Feminist Appraisal of the Influence of Menstruation on Women's Lives* (pp. 107–124). New York: Harrington Park Press.

Ad*Access On-Line Project. (n.d.). Ad #BH0017, John W. Hartman Center for Sales, Advertising & Marketing History, Duke University Rare Book, Manuscript, and Special Collections Library. Retrieved May 29, 2003, from http://scriptorium.lib.duke.edu/dynaweb/adaccess/beauty/ femhygiene1930s/@Generic_BookTextView/1062.

———. (n.d.). Ad #BH0019, John W. Hartman Center for Sales, Advertising & Marketing History, Duke University Rare Book, Manuscript, and Special Collections Library. Retrieved May 29, 2003, from http://scriptorium.lib .duke.edu/dynaweb/adaccess/beauty/femhygiene1930s/@Generic _BookTextView/1062.

———. (n.d.). Ad #BH0159, John W. Hartman Center for Sales, Advertising & Marketing History, Duke University Rare Book, Manuscript, and Special Collections Library. Retrieved May 29, 2003, from http://scriptorium.lib .duke.edu/dynaweb/adaccess/beauty/femhygiene1930s/@Generic _BookTextView/1062.

———. (n.d.). Ad #BH0229, John W. Hartman Center for Sales, Advertising & Marketing History, Duke University Rare Book, Manuscript, and Special Collections Library. Retrieved May 29, 2003, from http:// scriptorium.lib.duke.edu/dynaweb/adaccess/beauty/femhygiene1930s/@ Generic_BookTextView/1062.

———. (n.d.). Ad #BH0238, John W. Hartman Center for Sales, Advertising & Marketing History, Duke University Rare Book, Manuscript, and Special Collections Library. Retrieved May 29, 2003, from http:// scriptorium.lib.duke.edu/dynaweb/adaccess/beauty/femhygiene1920s/@ Generic_BookTextView/1974.

"Advertising: That's Very Interesting." (1994). *Marketing to Women,* July: 4.

Akin, Marjorie. (1996). "Passionate Possession." In W. David Kingery (ed.), *Learning from Things: Method and Theory of Material Culture Studies* (pp. 102–128). Washington, DC: Smithsonian Institution Press.

Ambrose, Timothy, and Crispin Paine. (1993). *Museum Basics*. London: ICOM/Routledge.

American Association of Museums (AAM). (2001). "Museum Advancement and Accreditation: Accreditation." Retrieved September 3, 2001, from http://www.aam-us.org/accred.htm.

American Psychiatric Association. (1994). *Diagnostic and Statistical Manual of Mental Disorders,* 4th edition. Washington, DC: American Psychiatric Association.

Anderson, F. D., and Howard Hait. (2003). "A Multicenter, Randomized Study of an Extended Cycle Oral Contraceptive." *Contraception* 68, no. 2: 89–96.

Anderson, Garnet L., Howard L. Judd, Andrew M. Kaunitz, David H. Barad, Shirley A. A. Beresford, Mary Pettinger, James Liu, Gene McNeeley, and Ana Maria Lopez. (2003). "Effects of Estrogen plus Progestin on Gynecologic Cancers and Associated Diagnostic Procedures. *Journal of the American Medical Association* 290: 1739–1748.

ARHP (Association of Reproductive Health Professionals). (2003). *Menstruation and Menstrual Suppression: What Women and Health Care Providers Really Think*. Washington, DC: ARHP. Retrieved November 30, 2003, from http://www.arhp.org/menstruation.

Armstrong, Liz, and Adrienne Scott. (1992). *Whitewash: Exposing the Health and Environmental Dangers of Women's Sanitary Products and Disposable Diapers*. Toronto: HarperCollins.

Asso, Doreen. (1983). *The Real Menstrual Cycle*. Chicester: John Wiley.

Atack, Margaret. (1998). "Writing from the Centre: Ironies of Otherness and Marginality." In Ruth Evans (ed.), *Simone de Beauvoir's* The Second Sex*: New Interdisciplinary Essays* (pp. 30–58). Manchester: Manchester University Press.

Avorn, Jerry. (2004). *Powerful Medicines: The Benefits, Risks, and Costs of Prescription Drugs*. New York: Knopf.

B., Ruth (2003). "Ruth's Page: Endometriosis and Dioxin." Retrieved May 15, 2003, from http://www.frontiernet.net/~ruthb/index.html.

Bailey, J. W., and L. S. Cohen. (1999). "Prevalence of Mood and Anxiety Disorders in Women Who Seek Treatment for Premenstrual Syndrome." *Journal of Women's Health and Gender Based Medicine* 8, no. 9: 1181–1184.

Bancroft, J. (1995). "The Menstrual Cycle and the Well Being of Women." *Social Science & Medicine* 41, no. 6: 785–791.

Bannett, Tracy. (1995). "S.P.O.T. The Tampon Health Website." Retrieved May 6, 2003, from http://www.spotsite.org.

Barr Laboratories. (2003). "Barr Begins Detailing Seasonale to Physicians and Healthcare Providers." Press release. November 18, Woodcliff Lake, NJ.

Beausang , C. C., and A. G. Razor, (2000). "Young Western Women's Experiences of Menarche and Menstruation." *Health Care for Women International* 21: 517–528.

Beauvoir, Simone de. (1952). *The Second Sex*. Translated by H. M. Parshley. New York: Vintage Books.

Berg, D. H., and L. Block Coutts. (1994). "The Extended Curse: Being a Woman Every Day." *Health Care for Women International* 15, no. 11: 11–22.

Berger, John. (1973). *Ways of Seeing*. London: BBC and Penguin.

Birnbaum, Linda S., and Audrey M. Cummings. (2002). "Dioxins and Endometriosis: A Plausible Hypothesis." *Environmental Health Perspectives* 110: 15- 21.

Blood Sisters. (n.d.) "The Blood Sisters Project: When the Private Becomes Public." Retrieved May 6, 2003, from http://bloodsisters.org/bloodsisters.

Bobel, Christina. (2003). "'Our Revolution Has Style': Contemporary Text-Based Menstrual Activism in the U.S." Paper presented at biannual meeting of the Society for Menstrual Cycle Research, Pittsburgh, PA.

Bogo, Jennifer. (2001). "Inner Sanctum: The Hidden Price of Feminine Hygiene Products." *E Magazine,* March/April. Retrieved July 25, 2002, from http://www.emagazine.com/march-april 2001/0301glhealth.html.

Boston Women's Health Collective. (1998). *Our Bodies, Ourselves for the New Century.* Boston: Simon & Schuster.

Boylan, Kristi Meisenbach. (2001). *The Seven Sacred Rites of Menarche: The Spiritual Journey of the Adolescent Girl.* Santa Monica, CA: Santa Monica Press.

Boys Don't Cry. (1999). Produced by J. Sharp, J. Hart, E. Kolodner, and C. Vachon, and directed by K. Pierce. Los Angeles: Fox Searchlight Pictures. Videotape.

Breggin, P. R. (2002). *Psychiatric Drug Facts.* Retrieved February 13, 2002, from www.breggin.com.

Breggin, P. R., and G. R. Breggin. (1994). *Talking Back to Prozac: What Doctors Won't Tell You About Today's Most Controversial Drug.* New York: St. Martin's Press.

Brooks-Gunn, J., and D. Ruble. (1980). "The Menstrual Attitude Questionnaire." *Psychosomatic Medicine* 42: 503–512.

————. (1980). "Menarche: The Interaction of Physiological, Cultural, and Social Factors." In A. J. Dan, E. A. Graham, and C. P. Beecher (eds.), *The Menstrual Cycle: A Synthesis of Interdisciplinary Research* (Volume 1) (pp. 141–159). New York: Springer.

Brumberg, Joan Jacobs. (1997). *The Body Project: An Intimate History of American Girls.* New York: Random House.

Brunvand, Jan Harold. (1981). *The Vanishing Hitchhiker: American Urban Legends And Their Meanings.* New York: Norton.

Buckley, Thomas, and Alma Gottlieb (eds.). (1988). *Blood Magic: The Anthropology of Menstruation.* Berkeley: University of California Press.

Burcaw, G. Ellis. (1983). *Introduction to Museum Work,* 2nd edition. Nashville, TN: American Association for State and Local History.

Butler, Judith. (1989). "Gendering the Body: Beauvoir's Philosophical Contribution." In Ann Garry and Marilyn Pearsall (eds.), *Women, Knowledge, and Reality: Explorations in Feminist Philosophy* (pp. 253–262). Boston: Unwin Hyman.

————. (1990). *Gender Trouble.* New York: Routledge.

Caplan, P. (1995). *They Say You're Crazy: How the World's Most Powerful Psychiatrists Decide Who's Normal.* Reading, MA: Addison-Wesley.

————. (2001). "'Premenstrual Mental Illness': The Truth About Sarafem." *Network News* 26, May/June.

————. (2002). "You, Too, Can Hold a Congressional Briefing: The SMCR Goes to Washington About 'Premenstrual Dysphoric Disorder' and Sarafem." *Society for Menstrual Cycle Research Newsletter* (Summer).

Retrieved December 15, 2005, from http://www.menstruationresearch
.org/resources/newsletters/summer-2002.

Carrie. (1976). Produced by B. De Palma, P. Monash, and L. A. Stroler, and
directed by B. DePalma. Los Angeles: United Artists. Videotape.

Centers for Disease Control. (1983). "Update: Toxic-Shock Syndrome—United
States." *MMWR Weekly* 32, no. 30 (August 5): 398–400. Retrieved May
13, 2003, from http://www.cdc.gov/mmwr/preview/mmwrhtml/00000119
.htm.

———. (1990). "Historical Perspectives Reduced Incidence of Menstrual
Toxic-Shock Syndrome—United States, 1980–1990." *MMWR Weekly* 39,
no. 25 (June 29): 421–423. Retrieved May 13, 2003, from http://www
.cdc.gov/mmwr/preview/mmwrhtml/00001651.htm.

Chesler, Giovanna. (2004). "Filmography. G6 Pictures. The Films of Giovanna Chesler." Retrieved August 17, 2005, from http://www.g6
pictures.com/filmography/filmography.htm.

———. (2005). Screening of *Period: The End of Menstruation?* Presentation at biannual meeting of the Society for Menstrual Cycle Research,
Boulder, CO.

Chrisler, Joan, Ingrid K. Johnston, Nicole M. Champagne, and Kathleen E.
Preston. (1994). "Menstrual Joy: The Construct and Its Consequences."
Psychology of Women Quarterly 18: 375–387.

Chrisler, Joan C., and Paula Caplan. (2002). "The Strange Case of Dr. Jekyll
and Ms. Hyde: How PMS Became a Cultural Phenomenon and a Psychiatric Disorder." *Annual Review of Sex Research* 13: 274–306.

Chrisler, Joan C., and C. B. Zittel. (1998). "Menarche stories: Reminis-
cences of college students from Lithuania, Malaysia, Sudan, and the
United States." *Health Care for Women International* 19: 303–312.

Clements, S. (2001). "The Name Changes, but the Drug Remains the Same:
Prozac vs Sarafem." 9News, KUSA TV, Denver. Retrieved November
27, 2001, from http://9news.com/health/sarafem.htm.

Condor, Bob. (2000). "Separating Fact from Quackery in Those Mass E-
mailings." [Electronic Version]. *Chicago Tribune,* July 12.

Cooper, Sherri. (2005). "Giving Up the Girl" (Episode #57). In Greg
Berlanti, Mickey Lidell, and Rina Mimoun (Executive Producers), *Everwood.* Everwood, UT: Berlanti/Liddell Productions. Television show.

Coutinho, Elsimar, with Sheldon Segal. (1999). *Is Menstruation Obsolete?*
New York: Oxford University Press.

Cox, Carol A. (2003). "FDA Approves Barr's Seasonale, an Extended-Cycle
Oral Contraceptive." Press Release, September 5. Woodcliff Lake, NJ:
Barr Laboratories.

Culpepper, E. (1991). "Menstruation Consciousness Raising: A Personal and
Pedagogical Process." In A. J. Dan and L. Lewis, (eds.), *Menstrual
Health in Women's Lives* (pp. 274–284). Urbana: University of Illinois
Press.

Cutler, Winnifred. (2002). "Menstrual Suppression by Contraception and
Non Cyclic Regimens of Hormonal Replacement Therapy Are Poten-
tially Dangerous to a Woman's Health." Athena Institute. Retrieved
October 21, 2003, from http://www.athenainstitute.com/media.html.

Dalton, Katharina. (1978). *Once a Month.* Glasgow: Fontana Paperbacks.

D'Angelo, Vinnie. (n.d.) "The Cases." Vinnie's Tampon Case. Retrieved July 13, 2004, from http://www.tamponcase.com.

Daw, Jennifer. (2002) "Is PMDD Real?" *Monitor on Psychology* 33, no. 9. Retrieved December 22, 2003, from http://www.apa.org/monitor/oct02/pmdd.html.

Delaney, Janice, Mary Jane Lupton, and Emily Toth. (1988). *The Curse: A Cultural History of Menstruation* (2nd ed.). Urbana: University of Illinois Press.

Dennett, Andrea Stulman. (1997). *Weird and Wonderful: The Dime Museum in America.* New York: New York University Press.

DeVito, Michael J., and Arnold Schecter. (2002). "Exposure Assessment to Dioxins from the Use of Tampons and Diapers." *Environmental Health Perspectives* 110: 23–28.

"Do We Need Lifestyle Drugs?" (2003). BBC News, January 3. Retrieved July 20, 2005, from http://news.bbc.co.uk/1/low/health/2624547.stm.

"Doctors Say They've Found Cause of Toxic Shock." (1985). *The Los Angeles Times,* June 6, p. 10.

Douglas, Mary. (1966). *Purity and Danger: An Analysis of the Concepts of Pollution and Taboo.* London: Routledge.

Douglass, Emily, and Kate Zaidan. (2004). "Tampaction Action Packet." Student Environmental Action Coalition. Philadelphia. Retrieved August 7, 2005, from http://tampaction.org.

"Drug Industry Most Profitable in U.S." (2001). *CNN.com,* November 30.

Dyer, Gillian. (1988). *Advertising as Communication.* London: Routledge.

Eagan, A. (1985). "The Selling of Premenstrual Syndrome: Who Profits from Making PMS 'the Disease of the 1980s'?" In S. Laws, V. Heys, and A. Eagan (eds.), *Seeing Red: The Politics of Premenstrual Tension* (pp. 80–89). London: Hutchinson.

Earle, Richard. (2000). *The Art of Cause Marketing.* New York: McGraw-Hill.

Eco-Logique. (2003). "Menstruation—From Menarche to Menopause." Eco-Logique.com. Retrieved May 29, 2003, from www.eco-logique.com/h-menstruation.htm.

Edson, Gary, and David Dean. (1996). *The Handbook for Museums.* London: Routledge.

Ehrenreich, Barbara, and Deirdre English. (1978). *For Her Own Good: 150 Years of the Experts' Advice to Women.* New York: Anchor Books.

Elson, Jean. (2002). "Manipulating Menstruation Is Misguided." *Newsday .com,* October 31. Retrieved October 31, 2002, from http://www.newsday .com/templates/misc/printstory.jsp?slug=ny%2Dvpels312985402oct31 &section=%2Fnews%2Fhealth.

Environmental Protection Agency. (1997). "The Pulp and Paper Industry, the Pulping Process, and Pollutant Releases to the Environment." Fact Sheet EPA-821-F-97-011. Washington, DC: Environmental Protection Agency Office of Water.

———. (2001). "Dioxin: Summary of the Dioxin Reassessment Science." Information Sheet 1. Washington, DC: EPA Office of Research and Development.

Evans, Ruth. (1998). "Introduction: *The Second Sex* and the Postmodern." In Ruth Evans (ed.), *Simone de Beauvoir's* The Second Sex*: New Interdisciplinary Essays* (pp. 1–30). Manchester: Manchester University Press.

"FDA Panel Recommends Fluoxetine for PMDD." (1999). *Psychiatric News,* December 3.

Figert, A. E. (1996). *Women and the Ownership of PMS: The Structuring of a Psychiatric Disorder.* New York: Aldine de Gruyter.

Finley, Harry. (1998). "A Menstrual Hut in Hawaii." Museum of Menstruation. Retrieved July 28, 2001, from http://www.mum.org/MenstHut.htm.

———. (2000a). "Museum of Menstruation and Women's Health." Retrieved October 7, 2000, from http://www.mum.org.

———. (2000b) "Function and Future of This Museum." Museum of Menstruation and Women's Health. Retrieved October 7, 2000, from http://www.mum.org/future.htm.

Fiske, J. (1992). *Understanding Popular Culture.* London and New York: Routledge.

Food and Drug Administration. (1995). Office of Regulatory Affairs Compliance Policy Guidelines Sec. 345.300 Menstrual Sponges (CPG 7124.24). Retrieved July 8, 2003, from http://www.fda.gov/ora/compliance_ref/cpg/cpgdev/cpg345-300.html.

———. (1999). "Tampons and Asbestos, Dioxin, & Toxic Shock Syndrome," Center for Devices and Radiological Health. Retrieved May 6, 2003, from http://www.fda.gov/cdrh/consumer/tamponsabs.html.

———. (2000). *FDA Approves Fluoxetine To Treat Premenstrual Dysphoric Disorder* (pp. 1–2). Rockville, MD: US Department of Health and Human Services.

Francia, Luisa. (1991). *Dragontime: Magic and Mystery of Menstruation.* Translated by Sasha Daucus. Woodstock, NY: Ash Tree Publishing.

Fried, Jennifer. (2003). "Off the Rag." *Salon.com,* November 24. Retrieved November, 25, 2003, from http://archive.salon.com/mwt/feature/2003/11/25/periods/index_np.html.

Fudge, Rachel. (2004). "The View from Madison Avenue: Girls Stink." *Bitch* 25: 16.

Fuentes, Annette. (2002). "Beyond Birth Control: The Pill Tackles New Duties." *New York Times,* May 7. Retrieved May 10, 2002, from http://www.nytimes.com/2002/05/07/health/womenshealth/07PILL.html.

Gadsby, J. E. (2001). "A Major Global Health Epidemic: A Presentation for the World Assembly for Mental Health." Retrieved February 13, 2002, from http://www.benzo.org.uk/jegwamh.htm.

Gallant, S. J., and J. A. Hamilton. (1988). "On a Premenstrual Psychiatric Diagnosis: What's in a Name?" *Professional Psychology: Research and Practice* 19, no. 3: 271–278.

Gallant, S. J., D. A. Popiel, D. M. Hoffman, P. Chakraborty, and J. A. Hamilton. (1992a). "Using Daily Ratings to Confirm Premenstrual Syndrome/Late Luteal Phase Dysphoric Disorder. Part I: Effects of Demand Characteristics and Expectations." *Psychosomatic Medicine* 54: 149–166.

——— (1992b). "Using Daily Ratings to Confirm Premenstrual Syndrome/Late Luteal Phase Dysphoric Disorder. Part II: What Makes a 'Real' Difference?" *Psychosomatic Medicine* 54: 167–181.

Gaudin, Nicolas. (2005). "IARC Monographs Programme Finds Combined Estrogen-Progestogen Contraceptives and Menopausal Therapy Are Carcinogenic to Humans." Press Release, July 29. Lyon, France: World Health Organization International Agency for Research on Cancer.

"Generic Substitution Issues." (2001). *National Pharmacy Compliance News.* Washington, DC: US Food and Drug Administration.

Gerbner, G. (1998). "Casting the American Scene. Fairness and Diversity in Television." Screen Actors Guild Report, December, Retrieved February 21, 2002, from http://www.sag.org/special/americanscene .html.

Gibbs, Lois Marie. (1995). *Dying from Dioxin: A Citizen's Guide to Reclaiming Our Health and Rebuilding Democracy.* Boston: South End Press.

Ginger Snaps. (2000). Directed by John Fawcett. Canada: TVA International. Motion picture.

Glenmullen, J. (2000). *Prozac Backlash.* New York: Simon & Schuster.

Goldman, Robert. (1992). *Reading Ads Socially.* London: Routledge.

Green, P. (1998). *Cracks in the Pedestal: Ideology and Gender in Hollywood.* Amherst: University of Massachusetts Press.

Greenberg, Lori. (n.d.). "Meet Vinnie: The Newest Face on Your Tampon Case." AdiosBarbie.com. Retrieved July 31, 2003, from http://adiosbarbie .com/bodyoutlaw/vinnie.html.

Gurevich, M. (1995). "Rethinking the Label: Who Benefits from the PMS Construct?" *Women & Health* 23, no. 2: 67–98.

gypsy. (2003). "The Tampaction Campaign & Why It's an Amazing Thing." *Threshold,* April. Student Environmental Action Campaign: Philadelphia, PA.

Haijeh, Rana A., Arthur Reingold, Alexis Weil, Kathleen Shutt, Anne Schuchat, and Bradley A. Perkins. (1999). "Toxic Shock Syndrome in the United States: Surveillance Update, 1979–1996." *Emerging Infectious Diseases* 5: 807–810.

Hall, Stuart. (n.d.). *Cultural Analysis.* Birmingham, UK: Centre for Contemporary Cultural Studies.

Hamilton, J. A., and S. J. Gallant. (1990). "Problematic Aspects of Diagnosing Premenstrual Phase Dysphoria: Recommendations for Psychological Research and Practice." *Professional Psychology: Research and Practice* 21, no. 1: 60–68.

Hampton, B. (1996.) "Anything You Want." In A. Spelling (Producer) and S. Weisman (Director), *7th Heaven.* Los Angeles: WB Network. Television show.

Havemann, Judith. (1987). "Uniform Rules Sought on Tampon Absorbency; FDA Moving Seven Years After First Deaths." *The Washington Post,* June 9, p. A19.

Havens, B., and I. Swenson. (1988). "Imagery Associated with Menstruation in Advertising Targeted to Adolescent Women." *Adolescence* 23: 89–97.

Health Keeper. (2003). "The Diva Cup Menstrual Solution." Retrieved July 2, 2003, from http://www.keeper.com.

Healy, D. (2000). "Psychopharmacology and the Government of the Self." Lecture delivered November 30 at University of Toronto, Toronto, Ontario. Retrieved July 28, 2005, from http://healyprozac.com/Academic Freedom/lecture.pdf.

———. (2004). *Let Them Eat Prozac: The Unhealthy Relationship Between the Pharmaceutical Industry and Depression.* New York: New York University Press.

Heard, Kenneth V., Joan C. Chrisler, Leigh Ann Kimes, and Holly N. Siegel. (1999). "Psychometric Evaluation of the Menstrual Joy Questionnaire." *Psychological Reports* 84: 135–136.

Hill, Daniel Delis. (2002). *Advertising to the American Woman 1900–1999.* Columbus: Ohio State University Press.

Hitchcock, Christine, and Jerilynn Prior. (2003). "Experiments and Opinions on Menstrual Suppression from the Scientific Literature." Paper presented at biannual meeting of the Society for Menstrual Cycle Research, Pittsburgh, PA.

Hoffman, Karen. (2003). "Foes Raise Red Flag Against Suppression of Menstruation." *Pittsburgh Post-Gazette,* June 24. Retrieved June 26, 2003, from http://post-gazette.com/healthscience/20030624hcycle2.asp.

Houppert, Karen. (1995). "Pulling the Plug on the Sanitary Protection Industry." *Village Voice* 40, no. 6: 31–40. Retrieved May 28, 2003, from http://critpath.org/~tracy/village.html.

———. (1999). *The Curse: Confronting the Last Unmentionable Taboo: Menstruation.* New York: Farrar, Straus and Giroux.

Hoyt, Alex, and Linda C. Andrist. (2003). "Women's Attitudes and Beliefs About Menstrual Suppression." Paper presented at biannual meeting of the Society for Menstrual Cycle Research, Pittsburgh, PA.

Huffington, A. (2000). "Prozac: Unsafe at Any Price." *Arianna Online,* October 23. Retrieved February 17, 2002, from www.ariannaonline.com/columns/files/102300.html.

Hughes, Ellen Roney. (1997). "The Unstifled Muse: The 'All in the Family' Exhibit and Popular Culture at the National Museum of American History." In Amy Henderson and Adrienne L. Kaeppler (eds.), *Exhibiting Dilemmas: Issues of Representation at the Smithsonian.* Washington, DC: Smithsonian Institution Press.

ICOM (International Council of Museums). (2001). "Development of the Museum Definition According to ICOM Statutes (1946–2001)." International Council of Museums. Retrieved July 12, 2001, from http://icom.museum/hist_def_eng.html.

Ikramuddin, Aisha. (1997). "Toxic Shock!: How Safe Are Feminine Hygiene Products?" *E magazine,* July/August: pp. 42–43.

James-Enger, Kelly. (2001). "Cancer Prevention Breakthrough?" *Redbook* 196, no. 3 (March): 32.

Jameson, Fredric (1984) "Postmodernism, or the Cultural Logic of Late Capitalism," *New Left Review* 146: 53–93.

Johnson, Sharlene K. (2001). "No More Periods?" *Ladies Home Journal* 118, no. 4 (April): 70.

Johnson, T. M. (1987). "Premenstrual Syndrome as a Western Culture-Specific Disorder." *Culture, Medicine and Psychiatry* 11: 337–356.

Johnston-Robledo, Ingrid, Jessica Barnack, and Stephanie Bye. (2003). "Menstrual Suppression in the Popular Press." Paper presented at biannual meeting of the Society for Menstrual Cycle Research, Pittsburgh, PA.

Johnston-Robledo, Ingrid, Jessica Barnack, and Stephanie Wares. (in press). "'Kiss Your Period Good-Bye': Menstrual Suppression in the Popular Press." *Sex Roles.*

Judge, M. (1999). "Aisle 8A." In M. Judge and G. Daniels (Producers), *King of the Hill*. Los Angeles: Fox Television. Television show.

Kachman, Geneva. (2000). Appearance on *Moral Court*. Television show.

———. (2001). "Holomenses and Holocaust: A Comparison of the Museum of Menstruation and Women's Health and the United States Holocaust Memorial Museum." Paper presented at biannual meeting of the Society for Menstrual Cycle Research, Avon, CT.

———. (2002). "MOLTXPERIMENT: A Tale of Two Tape Measures." Museum of the Menovulatory Lifetime. Retrieved July 29, 2003, from http://www.moltx.org/tame.html.

———. (2003a). "MOLT: Museum of the Menovulatory Lifetime." Retrieved July 29, 2003, from http://www.moltx.org.

———. (2003b). "Re: Seasonale in Salon.com." Message posted to the Society for Menstrual Cycle Research's SMCR-MBRS electronic mailing list, November 26.

Kachman, Geneva, Molly Strange, Janis Hunter-Paulk, Maryel Backstrom, and Daisy Decapite. (2000). *Celebrate Menstrual Monday*. Self-published. Poster.

Kalb, Claudia. (2003). "Farewell to 'Aunt Flo.'" *Newsweek* 141, no. 5: 48.

Kane, Kate. (1997). "The Ideology of Freshness in Feminine Hygiene Commercials." In Charlotte Brundson, Julie D'Acci, and Lynn Spiegel (eds.), *Feminist Television Criticism: A Reader* (pp. 290–299). Oxford: Clarendon Press.

Kaye, Joyce Rutter. (2001). "Sanitary chic." *Print* 55: 62–67.

Kelley, Tina. (2003). "New Pill Fuels Debate over Benefits of Fewer Periods." *New York Times,* October 14. Retrieved October 13, 2003, from http://www.nytimes.com/2003/10/14/health/14PILL.html.

Kilbourne, Jean. (1999). *Deadly Persuasion: Why Women and Girls Must Fight the Addictive Power of Advertising*. New York: Simon & Schuster.

Kimberly-Clark. (2003a). "Info. Answers. Chat." Retrieved May 17, 2003, from http://www.kotex.com.

———. (2003b). "Let's Talk." Kotex.com. Retrieved May 21, 2003, from http://www.kotex.com/na/talk/women/.

Kirk, S. A., and H. Kutchins. (1995). *The Selling of DSM: The Rhetoric of Science in Psychiatry*. New York: Aldine de Gruyter.

Kirsch, Irving, Thomas J. Moore, Alan Scoboria, and Sarah S. Nicholls. (2002). "The Emperor's New Drugs: An Analysis of Antidepressant Medication Data Submitted to the U.S. Food and Drug Administration." *Prevention & Treatment* 5, July. Retrieved December 22, 2003, from http://journals.apa.org/prevention/volume5/pre0050023a.html.

Kissling, E. A. (1996a). "Bleeding Out Loud: Communication About Menstruation." *Feminism & Psychology* 6: 481–504.

———. (1996b). "'That's Just a Basic Teen-age Rule': Girls' Linguistic Strategies for Managing the Menstrual Communication Taboo." *Journal of Applied Communication Research* 24: 292–309.

Knopper, Melissa. (2003). "Intimate Knowledge: A New York Congresswoman Wants To See Better Information Made Available for a Product that 73 Million American Women Use as Many as 16,000 Times During Their Menstrual Lifetimes." *Chicago Tribune,* February 7. Retrieved

February 28, 2003, from http://www.chicagotribune.com/features/women/chi-0030227-tampons-story,1,2592957.story?coll=chi-leisurewoman news-hed.

Koff, Elissa, Jill Rierdan, and Margaret L. Stubbs. (1990). "Conceptions and Misconceptions of the Menstrual Cycle." *Women & Health* 16, no. 3/4: 119–136.

Kowalski, R. M., and T. Chapple. (2000). "The Social Stigma of Menstruation: Fact or Fiction?" *Psychology of Women Quarterly* 24: 74–80.

Kramer, P. (1993). *Listening to Prozac.* New York: Penguin Books.

———. (2000). "Female Troubles." *The New York Times Magazine,* October 1.

Lander, L. (1988). *Images of Bleeding: Menstruation as Ideology.* New York: Orlando Press.

Langer, G. (2000). "Use of Antidepressants Is a Long-Term Practice." *abcnews.com.* Retrieved February 24, 2002, from http://abcnews.go.com/onair/WorldNewsTonight/poll000410.html.

Laws, S. (1985). "Who Needs PMT? A Feminist Approach to the Politics of Premenstrual Tension." In S. Laws, V. Hey, and A. Eagan (eds.), *Seeing Red: The Politics of Premenstrual Tension* (pp. 17–65). London: Hutchinson.

———. (1990). *Issues of Blood: The Politics of Menstruation.* London: Macmillan.

Leahy, Janet, Lore Kimbrough, and Gordon Gartrelle. (1990). "The Infantry Has Landed (and They've Fallen Off the Roof)." In Marcy Carsey (Executive Producer), *The Cosby Show.* Los Angeles: Carsey/Warner. Television show.

Leggiere, Phil. (2005). "Period Piece." *MediaPost's Online Media*, January. Retrieved August 8, 2005, from http://www.mediapost.com/PrintFriend.cfm?articleId=286338.

Levin, Miriam R. (2001). "Museums in a Developing World." Course syllabus, Case Western Reserve University.

Levine, B. E. (2001). *Commonsense Rebellion: Debunking Psychiatry, Confronting Society.* New York: Continuum.

Lewis, Shawn D. (2003). "3-Month Pill Makes Periods Periodic." *Detroit News,* October 23. Retrieved October 28, 2003, from http://www.detnews.com/2003/health/0310/23/e01-305061.htm.

Lewis & Clark College Womyn's Center. (2001). "Menstruation." LC Womyn's Center. Retrieved April 27, 2002, from http://www.lclark.edu/~womynctr/menstruation.html.

Lindsey, Marina. (1993). "With Strings Attached." *Buzzworm: The Environmental Journal* (May/June): 24, 80.

Lippman, Abby. (2004). "Women's Cycles up for Sale: Neo-medicalization and Women's Reproductive Health." *Canadian Women's Health Network Magazine* 6/7, no. 4/1.

Love, Susan. (2003). "Your Questions." SusanLoveMD.com, November 17. Retrieved November 28, 2003, from http://susanlovemd.com/faq/birth/birth-control-pill.html.

Lunapads.com. (2003). "Lunapads FAQ." Lunapads.com. Retrieved March 14, 2003, from http://www.lunapads.com/about/faq.html#4.

Lundgren-Gothlin, Eva. (1996). *Sex and Existence: Simone de Beauvoir's The Second Sex.* Translated by Linda Schenck. Hanover, NH: Wesleyan University Press/University Press of New England.

Lury, Celia. (1996). *Consumer Culture*. New Brunswick, NJ: Rutgers University Press.

MacLean, Stephen. (2003). "Asbestos, Dioxin in Tampons?" *Medical Post* 39, no. 13 (April 1): 29.

Maher, L. (2001). "Misleading Millions? How One Drug Company Is Making Dough off Your Period Each Month." *Chick Click: Society + Politics*. Retrieved November 27, 2001, from societypolitics.chickclick.com/articles/33912p1.html.

Maloney, Carolyn. (2003). "Protect Women from Dioxin and Toxic Shock Syndrome." Press Release, January 27. Washington, DC.

Mann, Laurie D. T. (1994) Review of *Soap opera: The Inside Story of Procter & Gamble,* by Alecia Swasy. Frequently Up-dated Web Sites. Retrieved September 5, 2001, from http://dpsinfo.com/essays/soapop.html.

"Marketing Madness: Drugs." (2001). *The Economist* 360 (July 21): 51.

MarketResearch.com. (2001). *The U.S. Market for Feminine Hygiene Products*. Abstract. New York: MarketResearch.com.

Martin, Emily. (1987). *The Woman in the Body: A Cultural Analysis of Reproduction*. Boston: Beacon.

———. (1988). "Premenstrual Syndrome: Discipline, Work, and Anger in Late Industrial Societies." In Thomas Buckley and Alma Gottlieb (eds.), *Blood Magic: The Anthropology of Menstruation* (pp. 161–181). Berkeley: University of California Press.

Martin, Kathleen. (2002). "Beyond the Plain Brown Wrapper: Finally, Marketers Are Being More Realistic in Ads for a Product Women Hate To Use." *Marketing Magazine* (July 1): 14.

Mattelart, Michéle. (1986). *Women, Media, and Crisis: Femininity and Disorder*. London: Comedia.

Matthews, K. (2001). "Creating More Diseases for Women." *Merge* (May/June).

McAllister, Matthew P. (1996). *The Commercialization of American Culture: New Advertising, Control and Democracy*. Thousand Oaks, CA: Sage.

McCarthy, Eliza. (2002). "No More Monthly Bills." *Elle* (August): 116.

McCullough, Marie. (2003). "Nature vs. Culture: Period-Stalling Drug Raises Questions." *Philadelphia Inquirer,* September 15, p. C-1.

McFarlane, J., C. L. Martin, and T. M. Williams. (1988). "Mood Fluctuations: Women Versus Men and Menstrual Versus Other Cycles." *Psychology of Women Quarterly* 12: 201–223.

McKeaney, G. (1989). "Nightmare on Oak Street" In G. S. Maffeo (Producer) and J. Pasquin (Director), *Roseanne*. Los Angeles: Carsey/Werner. Television show.

Meinersmann, K. M. S. (1995). "Being and Becoming Menstruating Women: A Heideggerian Hermeneutical Analysis of the Stories of Women." Unpublished doctoral dissertation, Georgia State University.

Miles, Steven. (1998). *Consumerism—As a Way of Life*. London: Sage.

Mills, D. Shepperson, and M. Vernon. (1999). *Endometriosis: A Key to Healing Through Nutrition*. Shaftesbury, Dorset, UK: Element.

Mind Branch. (2003). *The Lifestyle Drugs Outlook to 2008: Unlocking New Value in Well-Being*. Mindbranch.com Catalog. Retrieved July 20, 2005, from http://mindbranch.com/catalog.

Mintzes, Barbara. (2002). "Direct to Consumer Advertising Is Medicalising Normal Human Experience." *British Medical Journal* 324: 908–909.

Moos, R. (1968). "The Development of a Menstrual Distress Questionnaire." *Psychosomatic Medicine* 30: 853–867.

Moynihan, R. (2004). "Controversial Disease Dropped from Prozac Product Information." *British Medical Journal* 328: 365.

Moynihan, R., and A. Cassels. (2005). *Selling Sickness: How the World's Biggest Pharmaceutical Companies Are Turning Us All into Patients.* New York: Nation Books.

Moynihan, R., I. Heath, and David Henry. (2002). "Selling Sickness: The Pharmaceutical Industry and Disease Mongering." *British Medical Journal* 324: 886–891.

My Girl. (1991). Produced by B. Grazer and directed by H. Zieff. Los Angeles: Columbia Pictures. Videotape.

National Cancer Institute. (2003). "Cancer Facts." November 3. Retrieved July 20, 2005, from http://cis.nci.nih.gov/fact/3_13.htm.

National Institutes of Health National Heart, Lung, and Blood Institute. (2002). "NHLBI Stops Trial of Estrogen Plus Progestin Due to Increased Breast Cancer Risk, Lack of Overall Benefit." Press Release, July 9. Washington, DC: NIH.

———. (2004). "NIH Asks Participants in Women's Health Initiative Estrogen-Alone Study to Stop Study Pills, Begin Follow-Up Phase." Press Release, March 2. Washington, DC: NIH.

National Women's Health Network. (2003). "Statement on Using an Extended Cycle of Oral Contraceptive Pill for Menstrual Suppression (Seasonale)," September. Washington, DC: National Women's Health Network.

Natracare. (n.d.) "100% Organic Tampons." Natracare. Retrieved May 12, 2003, from http://www.natracare.com/tampons.htm.

Newman, K. (2000). "Prozac Backlash: Long-Term Consequences for Taking Antidepressants Are Virtually Unknown." *abcnews.com.* Retrieved February 24, 2002, from abcnews.go.com/onair/CloserLokk/wnt000410 CL antidepressants feature.html.

Nichols, Sarah. (1995). "Positive Premenstrual Experiences—Do They Exist?" *Feminism & Psychology* 5, no. 2: 162–169.

Norcross, Eric. (1999). The Toaster Foundation. Retrieved September 3, 2001, from http://www.toaster.org.

Northrup, Christiane. (1998). *Women's Bodies, Women's Wisdom.* New York: Bantam.

O'Grady, Kathleen. (2002). "Is Menstruation Obsolete?" *The Canadian Women's Health Network.* Retrieved October 31, 2002, from http://www.cwhn.ca/resources/menstruation/obsolete.html.

Oler, Tammy. (2003). "Blood-Letting: Female Adolescence in Modern Horror Films." *Bitch* 21: 44–51.

Organic Essentials. 2003. Frequently Asked Questions. Retrieved July 7, 2003, from http://www.organicessentials.com/faq.html.

Ouellette, Laurie. (1991). "That Time of the Month." *Utne Reader* 46 (July/August): 34–36.

Owen, Lara. (1991). "The Sabbath of Women." *Whole Earth Review* (Summer): 84–91.

Pandora Pads. (2003). "Menstrual Sponge: 'Re-usable Silk Sponge Tampons.'" Pandora Pads. Retrieved May 11, 2003, from http://www.pandorapads.com/sponge.htm.

Park, Shelley M. (1996). "From Sanitation to Liberation?: The Modern and Postmodern Marketing of Menstrual Products." *Journal of Popular Culture* 30: 149–167.

Parry, Vince. (2003). "The Art of Branding a Condition." *Medical Marketing & Media* (May): 43–49.

Petersen, Melody. (2002). "New Medicines Seldom Contain Anything New, Study Finds." *New York Times*, May 29. Retrieved May 29, 2002, from http://www.nytimes.com/2002/05/29/business/29DRUG.html.

Philbin, Gail Schmoller. (2003). "New Pill Makes Periods a Quarterly Event." *Chicago Tribune,* June 4, p. 7.

"Pill Puts Periods on Hold." (2003). *Detroit Free Press,* October 3.

Pope, A. (2001). *The Wild Genie: The Healing Power of Menstruation.* Bowral, Australia: Sally Milner Publishing.

Potter, Linda S. (2001). "Menstrual Regulation and the Pill." In Etienne van de Walle and Elisha P. Renne (eds.), *Regulating Menstruation: Beliefs, Practices, Interpretations* (pp. 141–154). Chicago: University of Chicago Press.

Preston, Elizabeth H., and Cindy L. White. (2003). "What's Wrong with You?: Gendered Constructions of Illness and Normalcy in Direct-to-Consumer Advertisements for Prescription Antidepressant Drugs." Paper presented at annual meeting of the National Communication Association, November, Miami Beach, FL.

Preziosi, Donald. (1995). "Museology and Museography." *The Art Bulletin* 77, no. 1: 13–15.

Prior, Jerilynn. (2000). "Ovulatory Menstrual Cycles Are Not a Problem: Go with the Flow!" *The BC Endocrine Research Foundation Newsletter* 2, no. 2: 1–4, 8.

———. (2004a). "Re: Amenorrhea from long-OC is not likely to prevent breast cancer." Message posted to the Society for Menstrual Cycle Research's SMCR-MBRS electronic mailing list, March 5.

———. (2004b). "What Does the Menstrual Cycle Tell Us About Bone Health?" Paper presented at The Menstrual Cycle is a Vital Sign: A Scientific Forum, September 21, New York.

Procter & Gamble. (2003). "Tampon questions." Retrieved May 17, 2003, from http://www.tampax.com/en_us/pages/ques_main.shtml?pageid=tp0005.

Profet, Margie. (1993). "Menstruation as a Defense Against Pathogens Transported by Sperm." *The Quarterly Review of Biology* 68: 335–386.

Quinion, Michael. (1998). "Lifestyle Drug." *World Wide Words*. Retrieved July 20, 2005, from http://www.worldwidewords.org/turnsofphrase/tp-tif1.htm.

Raappana, Saara Myrene. (n.d.) "Thank God It's That Time of the Month . . . an Interview with Vinnie the Tampon Case Distributor." *Actionman Magazine*. Retrieved July 31, 2003, from http://www.actionmanmagazine.com/article_standard.php?article_id=215.

Rako, Susan. (2003). *No More Periods? The Risks of Menstrual Suppression and Other Cutting-Edge Issues About Hormones and Women's Health.* New York: Harmony Books.

Ratliff, Darci (aka Kittenpants) and Lisa Johnson (aka FoxBox). (n.d.). "Interview: Vinnie!" *Kittenpants.com.* Retrieved July 31, 2003, from http://www.kittenpants.org/22_dingdong/vinnie.asp.

Research and Forecasts, Inc. (1981). *The Tampax Report: Summary of Survey Results on a Study of Attitudes Towards Menstruation.* New York: Research and Forecasts.

Rittenhouse, C. A. (1991). "The Emergence of Premenstrual Syndrome as a Social Problem." *Social Problems* 38, no. 3: 412–425.

Roberts, T.-A. (2004). "Female Trouble: The Menstrual Self-Evaluation Scale and Women's Self-Objectification." *Psychology of Women Quarterly* 28: 22–26.

Roberts, T.-A., J. Goldenberg, C. Power, and T. Pyszczynski. (2002). "'Feminine Protection': The Effects of Menstruation on Attitudes Toward Women." *Psychology of Women Quarterly* 26: 131–139.

Rodin, M. (1992). "The Social Construction of Premenstrual Syndrome." *Social Science & Medicine* 35, no. 1: 49–56.

Rome, Esther R., and Jill Wolhandler. (1991). "Can Tampon Safety Be Regulated?" In Alice J. Dan and Linda L. Lewis (eds.), *Menstrual Health in Women's Lives* (pp. 261–273). Urbana: University of Illinois Press.

Rosendahl, I. (1995). "Menstruation Taboos Falling by the Wayside." *Drug Topics* 139 (April 24): 42.

Rowland, R. (2002). "FDA Signs Off on Zoloft for Extreme PMS." *CNN.com,* May 21. Retrieved May 22, 2002, from http://www.cnn.com/2002/HEALTH/conditions/05/21/zoloft.pms/index.html.

Samuelson, Joan Benoit, and Gloria Averbuch. (1995). *Joan Samuelson's Running for Women.* Emmaus, PA: Rodale Press.

Sanacore, Frank K. (2003). "Pharmacotherapies for Depression and Other Conditions." *Drug Topics* 147, no. 16: 55.

Sanger, Margaret. (1920). *Woman and the New Race.* New York: Brentanos. Retrieved August 13, 2005, from http://bartleby.com/1013/.

Satish, Medapati, and R. Mathangi Sri. (2005). "Brand Cult." Department of Management Studies, National Institute of Technology, Tiruchirappalli, India. Retrieved December 14, 2005, from http://www.nitt.edu/departments/mba/Resources/Matsat1.html.

Schneider, Mary Ellen. (2004). "Menstrual Suppression—Policy & Practice." *OB/GYN News,* January 14. Retrieved August 19, 2005, from http://findarticles.com/p/articles/mi_m0CYD/is_2_39/ai113138541.

Scialli, Anthony R. (2001). "Tampons, Dioxin, and Endometriosis." *Reproductive Toxicology* 15: 231–238.

Scott, Ben. (2001). "Beer." In Richard Maxwell (ed.), *Culture Works: The Political Economy of Culture* (pp. 60–82). Minneapolis: University of Minnesota Press.

Seaman, Barbara. (2003). *The Greatest Experiment Ever Performed on Women: Exploding the Estrogen Myth.* Hyperion: New York.

Shanker, Wendy. (2002). "Padding It." *Grace* (Summer): 50.

Shaw, Joan Fern. (1988). "A Period of Quiet but Colorful Protest." In Dena Taylor, *Red Flower: Rethinking Menstruation.* Freedom, CA: The Crossing Press.

Sheehan, T. (1998). "Something About the 'Men' in Menstruation." In M. Govons (Producer) and M. Tash (Director), *Something So Right.*

Los Angeles: Big Phone Productions/Universal Television. Television show.

Siegel, Robert, and Rachel Jones. (2003). "Analysis: Ethical Implications and Potential Risks of Seasonale." *NPR: All Things Considered,* September 29. Washington, DC: National Public Radio. Radio broadcast.

Signorelli, N. (1997). "A Content Analysis: Reflections of Girls in the Media: A Study of Television Shows and Commercials, Movies, Music Videos, and Teen Magazine Articles and Ads." Kaiser Family Foundation, April. Retrieved February 21, 2002, from http://www.kff.org/content/archive/1260/gendr.html.

Silbergeld, Ellen. (1992). The Human Health Effects of Dioxin and Ongoing Scientific Assessment of Risk. Hearing before the Human Resources and Intergovernmental Relations Subcommittee of the House Committee on Government Operations, 102d Cong., 2d Sess. Washington, DC: US Government Printing Office.

Silverstein, Ken. (1999). "Millions for Viagra, Pennies for Diseases of the Poor." *The Nation,* July 19. Retrieved July 21, 2004, from http://www.thenation.com/mhtml?I=19990719&s=silverstein.

Singer, Michelle A. L. (2001). "Top 10 Things To Know About Menstruation." Retrieved May 6, 2003, from http://www.lclark.edu/~womynctr/Top10Things.html.

Sivulka, Juliann. (1998). *Soap, Sex, and Cigarettes: A Cultural History of American Advertising.* Belmont, CA: Wadsworth.

Society of Obstetricians and Gynaecologists of Canada. (n.d.). "Hormone Replacement Therapy—Your Questions Answered." Retrieved December 20, 2003, from http://sogc.medical.org/pub_ed/tearDownMyth/page5_e.shtml.

Span, P. (1993). "Vicious Cycle: The Politics of Periods." *The Washington Post,* July 8, p. C-01.

Spartos, C. (2000). "Sarafem Nation." *Village Voice,* December 6–12.

Spitzer, R. L., J. B. W. Williams, M. B. First, and M. Gibbon. (n.d.). *Biometrics Research.* New York: Columbia University.

Steinem, Gloria. (1978). "If Men Could Menstruate." *Ms.* (October).

———. (1990). "Sex, Lies, and Advertising." *Ms.* 1, no. 1: 18–28.

Steiner, Andy. (2001). "Tussle over Tampons." *Utne Reader* 106: 32–34.

Stockbridge, L. L. (2000). "RE: NDA #18-936, Sarafem (fluoxetine HCI) Tablets, MACMIS #6523," Letter to Gregory T. Brophy, Director, US Regulatory Affairs, Eli Lilly and Company. Rockville, MD: Department of Health and Human Services.

Stolberg, Sheryl Gay. (2005). "House Rejects Coverage of Impotence Pills." *New York Times,* June 25. Retrieved June 26, 2005, from http://nytimes.com/2005/06/25/politics/25viagra.html.

Strassmann, Beverly. (1996). "The Evolution of Endometrial Cycles and Menstruation." *The Quarterly Review of Biology* 71: 181–220.

———. (1999). "Menstrual Synchrony Pheromones: Cause for Doubt." *Human Reproduction* 14, no. 3: 579–580.

Taflinger, R. (1996). "Domcom: Character-Based Situation Comedies Plot, Thought, Diction, Music, Spectacle." In *Sitcom: What It Is, How It Works.* Self-published, May 28. Retrieved October 6, 2000, from http://www.wsu.edu:8080/~taflinge/domcom.html.

Taylor, Dena. (1988). *Red Flower: Rethinking Menstruation.* Freedom, CA: Crossing Press.

Tierno, Philip M. (2001). *The Secret Life of Germs: Observations and Lessons from a Microbe Hunter.* New York: Pocket Books.

Tiggermann, Marika, and Christine Lewis. (2004). "Attitudes Toward Women's Body Hair: Relationship with Disgust Sensitivity." *Psychology of Women Quarterly* 28: 381–387.

Tracy, James F. (2004). "Between Discourse and Being: The Commodification of Pharmaceuticals in Late Capitalism." *The Communication Review* 7: 15–34.

Treneman, A. (1989). "Cashing in on the Curse: Advertising and the Menstrual Taboo." In L. Gamman and M. Marshment (eds.), *The Female Gaze: Women As Viewers of Popular Culture* (pp. 153–165). Seattle, WA: Real Comet Press.

Tsao, Amy. (2002). "Freedom from the Menstrual Cycle?" *Business Week Online,* May 23. Retrieved from http://www.businessweek.com/print/technology/content/may2002/tc20020523 4148.htm.

Tuana, Nancy. (1996). "Fleshing Gender, Sexing the Body: Refiguring the Sex/Gender Distinction." *The Southern Journal of Philosophy* 35 (Supplement): 53–71.

US House. (2001). Robin Danielson Act H.R. 360, 107th Cong., 1st Sess. Retrieved June 1, 2003, from http://thomas.loc.gov/cgi-bin/query/z ?c107:H.R.360:.

————. (2003). Robin Danielson Act H.R. 373 IH, 108th Congress. Retrieved May 10, 2003, from http://thomas.loc.gov/cgi-bin/query/z?c108:H.R .373.

Vendantam, S. (2001). "Renamed Prozac Fuels Women's Health Debate." *The Washington Post,* April 29, p. A-1.

Vintges, Karen. (1996). *Philosophy As Passion: The Thinking of Simone de Beauvoir.* Translated by Anne Lavelle. Bloomington: Indiana University Press.

A Walk on the Moon. (1999). Produced by D. Hoffman and directed by T. Goldwyn. New York: Miramax Films. Videotape.

Walker, Alice. (1983). "Only Justice Can Stop a Curse." In Barbara Smith (ed.), *Home Girls: A Black Feminist Anthology* (pp. 339–342). New York: Kitchen Table: Women of Color Press.

Wallace, Diana. (2003). "Let's Get One Thong Straight." *AlterNet,* January 30. Retrieved February 4, 2003, from http://www.alternet.org/story .html?StoryID=15065.

Weiner, Richard. (2004). "A Candid Look at Menstrual Products—Advertising and Public Relations." *Public Relations Quarterly* 49, no. 2: 26–28.

Westphal, Sylvia Pagan. (2002). "Lifting the Curse." *New Scientist,* March 16, pp. 38–41.

Wildavsky, Aaron, and Brendon Swedlow. (1995). "Dioxin, Agent Orange, and Times Beach." In Aaron Wildavsky (ed.) *But Is It True? A Citizen's Guide to Environmental Health and Safety Issues* (pp. 81–125). Cambridge, MA: Harvard University Press.

Williamson, Judith. (1978). *Decoding Advertisements: Ideology and Meaning in Advertising.* London: Marion Boyars.

Wood, Julia. (1998). *Gendered Lives: Communication, Gender, and Culture,* 3rd edition. Belmont, CA: Wadsworth.

Woods, Nancy Fugate. (2005). "Women's Health Research: What's New?" Keynote address at biannual meeting of the Society for Menstrual Cycle Research, Boulder, CO.

Yanello, Amy. (1998). "Convenience or Health Threat?" *The Press-Tribune* (Roseville, CA), May 6. Retrieved April 29, 2003, from http://www .frontiernet.net/~ruthb/page3.html.

Young, M. (2001). "PMS and PMDD: Identification and Treatment." *Patient Care* 35, no. 2: 29–50.

Young, Stephen A., Nioaka Campbell, and Angela Harper. (2002). "Depression in Women of Reproductive Age: Considerations in Selecting Safe, Effective Therapy." *Postgraduate Medicine* 112, no. 3: 45.

Index

About the Book

ALTHOUGH A REGULAR OCCURRENCE FOR MILLIONS OF WOMEN, menstruation is typically represented in US culture as an illness or a shameful episode—to the benefit of an entire industry. Elizabeth Kissling reveals how corporations capitalize on long-standing negative attitudes about menses to sell solutions for nonexistent problems.

The commercialization of menstruation, Kissling acknowledges, has in many ways been positive: women embrace readily available, reasonably priced, and easy-to-use products with good reason. But it has also been one of the worst things to happen to women. Documenting how industry advertising portrays women as "the weaker sex," Kissling explores the profound gender bias inherent in—and reinforced by—the business of menstruation.

Elizabeth Arveda Kissling is professor of communication and women's studies at Eastern Washington University. She has written widely on menarche and menstruation.